five days in october

University of Missouri Press
Columbia

five days in october

The Lost Battalion of World War I

Robert H. Ferrell

Library of Congress Cataloging-in-Publication Data

Ferrell, Robert H.
    Five days in October : the Lost Battalion of World War I /
Robert H. Ferrell.
        p. cm.
    Summary: "Examination of the World War I battle of October
1918, in the Argonne Forest between German forces and the
Lost Battalion from the American Seventy-seventh Division.
Utilizes the papers of General Hugh A. Drum and other sources
to reexamine the heroic survival of Major Charles W. Whittlesey
and his troops"—Provided by publisher.
    Includes bibliographical references and index.
    ISBN 978-0-8262-2073-8 (alk. paper)
    1. United States. Army. Division, 77th—History. 2. Argonne,
Battle of the, France, 1918. 3. World War, 1914–1918—Regimental
histories—United States. I. Title.
    D570.377th .F47 2005
    940.4'36—dc22
                                                    2005001231

Designer: Kristie Lee
Typefaces: Veljovic and Windsor Antique
Jacket photos courtesy National Archives

contents

It was the most poignant incident of the American part in the World War, and its biggest newspaper story.

—Thomas M. Johnson, "The Lost Battalion,"
American Magazine 108 (November 1929): 54

preface

No single action of the U.S. Army in France in World War I re-ceived such attention, both within the American high command and from newspaper accounts throughout the country. One hun-dred million Americans, people said, knew about it (the country had reached a population of one hundred million in 1915). The valor of the surrounded troops during the great battle of the Meuse-Argonne in 1918 seemed comparable to that of the men of the Alamo and to the force of George A. Custer at the Little Big Horn. The whole af-fair was memorable when other events of the war blurred and be-came almost forgotten; Americans could not forget what it meant for five hundred men surrounded in the Argonne Forest to fight for five days, fired upon morning to night by riflemen, machine guns, mortars, and on occasion artillery, with nothing to eat after the morn-ing of the first day save grass and roots—what it meant to defy the German foe until relief at last came. The commander of the em-battled troops, a tall, lanky, bespectacled New York lawyer, Major Charles W. Whittlesey, said that when the men heard the whine of the Springfields, the distinctive sound of Chauchat submachine guns, in the hands of the relieving 307th Infantry Regiment, becoming ever louder, ever closer, it was like the bagpipes of the relieving British force approaching Lucknow during the Sepoy Rebellion.

It was said at the time and later that the Lost Battalion was nei-ther lost nor a battalion, and this was true, but the bravery of the American defenders was not lessened by such facts. On the days after the troops went into what soon was described as a pocket, on the reverse slope of a hill, part of a valley in the Argonne, their commander, Whittlesey, released six pigeons, carrying a series of accounts of his plight with the men. Each message contained his coordinates, 294.6–276.3. All of the birds got through, and within minutes their information was known to the division commander and staff; to the commander of the 154th Infantry Brigade, under whom were two regiments, one of them the 308th Infantry, that of the Lost Battalion; and to the division's artillery brigade commander. Everyone knew where the men were; there is no question of that. A newspaper editor in New York, learning that a sizable body of troops had been surrounded, thought up the notion of a Lost Battalion—it possessed a ring, sure to catch the attention of readers. He cabled back to his correspondent in France to "send more on Lost Battalion."

The troops similarly were not a battalion, but two, together with sections from the brigade machine-gun battalion. Whittlesey commanded the First Battalion of the 308th Infantry—there were three battalions in the regiment and his was the attack battalion. The commander of the other battalion that went into the pocket with Whittlesey was a captain, and the major was the senior man. In addition, the morning after the battalions arrived at the valley, Company K came in, from the 307th Infantry. And then, as mentioned, there were the machine-gun men, who brought in nine heavy Hotchkiss guns, which Whittlesey put on both ends of his force to ward off attacks from right and left.

The men belonged to the U.S. Seventy-seventh or "Liberty" Division, a New York City National Army, or draft, division. But the men of the Lost Battalion were by no means all New Yorkers, for the division had been in the Oise-Aisne country beginning in mid-August, and the losses of that campaign had brought in replacements. The latter came from the American West, from California, Utah, Arizona, and Colorado.

It is a point of interest that the men of the Seventy-seventh, chosen for the Argonne, which area was only a small part of the twenty-mile American front in the battle known as the Meuse-Argonne, possessed no acquaintance with the terrain they encountered where they were involved in virtual Indian fighting. They were totally unacquainted with the tangle of trees and bushes, of ravines beyond end and in some places hills that approached the definition of cliffs, that composed the Argonne Forest. In September 1918, the Seventh-

seventh first moved up into this God-forsaken country. In the sometimes peculiar American Army way—the U.S. Army has a saying,
that there is a right way and a wrong way and the army way—they
were chosen for the equivalent of the terrain of the Old Northwest,
as the present-day Middle West was once known.

Whittlesey was the commander of the troops, and his was a personality to remember. He had been brought up in New England, and
when he became a national figure, known like his men to millions
of readers, newspapermen described him as possessing the typical
reserve of individuals from his region. Laconic he indeed was, and
not in the least inclined to talk about himself. Because of his tragic
suicide three years later it is entirely possible that even then, in 1918,
something was concerning him, that there were feelings larger than
fighting and warfare, that somehow the task that lay before him
when he was in the Argonne was distasteful, if necessary, and the
former appraisal eventually got the better of the latter. Of that, to be
sure, no one really could tell, whatever it is tempting to conclude.
Best it may be to say that Charles Whittlesey was a private person,
one who did not wear his thoughts on his sleeve.

Whittlesey's second in command, Captain George G. McMurtry,
was quite the opposite. Short, stocky, ebullient—always cheerful—
McMurtry was full of the latest pat phrases, such as something or
other being "red hot." Like Whittlesey he came from New York City
and had been a stockbroker. He graduated in the Harvard class of
1899, leaving temporarily in 1898 to join the Rough Riders in Cuba,
that marvelous organization of Harvard men and cowboys with its
colonel Leonard Wood, its lieutenant colonel (some thought the colonel) Theodore Roosevelt.

Major Whittlesey and Captain McMurtry were different in their
ways, but in one quality they were the same. They were individuals
of resolution; there was steel in those two officers. They were the
right sort to do what they were instructed to do and if necessary
take men into a difficult place and hold it, against all odds.

acknowledgments

Once again it is a pleasure to thank the staff of the modern military branch of the National Archives in College Park, Maryland: Timothy R. Nenninger, chief of the branch, and especially Mitchell A. Yockelson, the World War I archivist. Similarly, Richard J. Sommers and David A. Keough, head of the search room and archivist of the U.S. Army Military History Institute, a part of the Army War College at Carlisle Barracks, Carlisle, Pennsylvania. A thank-you to the archivist, Jonathan R. Casey, and curator, Doran L. Cart, of the Liberty Memorial in Kansas City, and to the director of the museum, Eli Paul. Larry I. Bland provided the diary of Pierpont L. Stackpole, and Edward M. Coffman the memoir of George B. Duncan. David K. Frasier and Jeffrey C. Graf of the Indiana University Library in Bloomington searched out references in the *New York Times* and *Los Angeles Times.*

Betty Bradbury was the word processor. John M. Hollingsworth was the cartographer.

It is so helpful to work with Beverly Jarrett, director and editor-in-chief, Jane Lago, managing editor, and Kristie Lee, designer, of the University of Missouri Press. The director brought her infectious enthusiasm, Jane Lago expertly did the editing, and Kristie Lee made the resultant book look right.

James J. Cooke and Bruce Clayton were readers for the press and caught me up on errors small and large. I am indebted to John Lukacs the historian for equally wise counsel.

Carolyn and Lorin make everything easier.

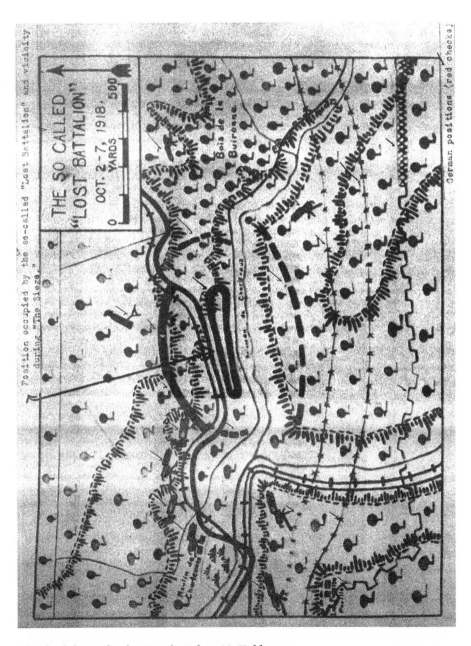

Sketch of the pocket by Captain Nelson M. Holderman.

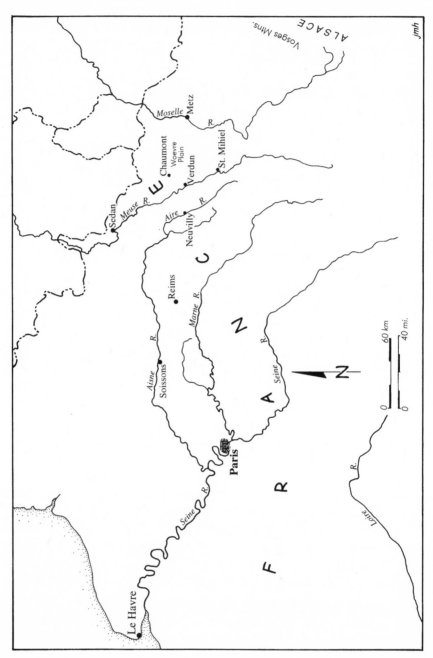

Northern France.

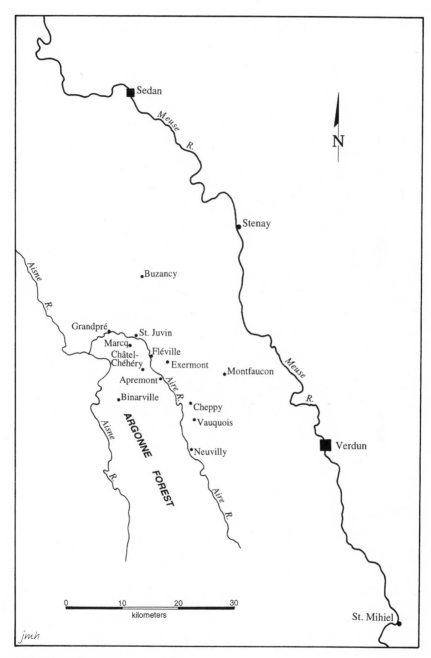

The Meuse-Argonne.

XV

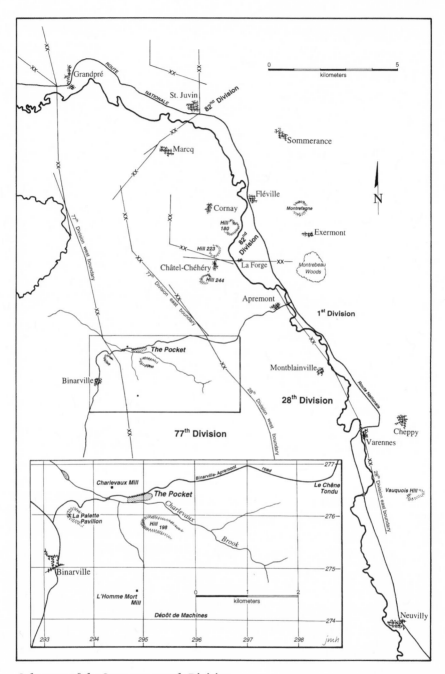

Subsector of the Seventy-seventh Division.

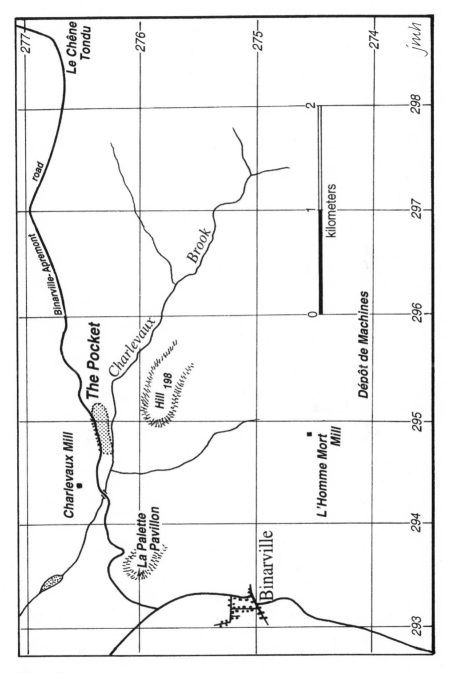

The pocket.

five days in october

one Causes

The question at the outset is how the commander of the American Expeditionary Forces, the AEF, General John J. Pershing, and the commander of the Seventy-seventh Division, Major General Robert Alexander, allowed the companies of the Lost Battalion to be trapped and suffer their heroic days of tragic losses. How were the men allowed to come to the edge of surrender?

Personalities are not usually a fair way to explain historical events. Yet, in searching for the causes of the predicament of the Lost Battalion, it is of advantage to see the forces and factors of its entrapment in terms of the commanders in the field, in this case Pershing and Alexander. This does not mean that they encapsulated everything in a complex equation, for they assuredly did not. But without discussion of what they were up against, and how they reacted, the plight of the Lost Battalion shades off into geography and perhaps inevitability, neither of which explains what happened on October 2–7, 1918.

Of the two personalities, the one bearing most responsibility for what the AEF did, and perhaps did not do, was Pershing, a fine figure of a man in his well-fitting uniform and with his regulation cap, the four stars of a full general on each of his broad shoulders. Born in Missouri in the last year before the Civil War, 1860, he had an army career both typical and untypical of AEF generals in 1917–1918.

The background of the man who after the war received the title of General of the Armies, and who lived on for many years in partial and then full retirement, dying in the faraway year of 1948, was at the outset unremarkable.[1] Like a few other American youths of his era—there were not many, for West Point, to which he went in 1882, a bit old for his classmates, was a small place, enrolling fewer than three hundred cadets—he chose the army for a career. At that time a career in the military no longer was attractive. The Indian rebellions for a while had offered opportunities for military experience, but those were petering out, with some fighting against the Apaches in the Southwest but little else seemingly available that would interrupt the dull garrison life in the small posts scattered, largely by political choice, across the country.

A few years after graduation in the class of 1886, of which he was cadet first captain, at the military but not intellectual head of his class, Pershing went out to Lincoln, Nebraska, where he was commandant of cadets at the state college. There he earned a law degree. He was accustomed to eating at Don Cameron's fifteen-cent lunch counter with two other young men, one of whom was a rotund lawyer with political ambition by the name of William J. Bryan. The other was an equally ambitious lawyer, Charles G. Dawes, who would serve as vice president of the United States from 1925 to 1929. Discouraged by his prospects in the army, in his midthirties, and still a lieutenant, Pershing one day inquired of Dawes whether he should quit the army and become a lawyer. "I'd try the army for a while yet," said Dawes.

The coming of the war with Spain did nothing for Pershing, not even promoting him to captain, which rank he received in 1901. After that three-month conflict, which was hardly a war, Pershing, like nearly all of the Regulars, went out to the Philippines, where the task was to pacify the rebellious islanders. In this he excelled, for he possessed the firmness and resolution for which he later became famous. And in his ability to put down the Moro tribes in their private rebellion, which continued for several years after 1898, he came to the attention of President Roosevelt, who said that Pershing was the best man in the army, and "by George" he was going to do something for him. It did not harm Captain Pershing's prospects that his father-in-law was Francis E. Warren, a senator from Wyoming and chairman of the military affairs committee. Impulsively, with the calculation that "T.R." often showed that was a part of his genius, the president promoted Pershing to brigadier general, infuriating hundreds, indeed 862, of Pershing's senior officers who were passed over with what amounted to a Rooseveltian snort of impatience.

By the time of the shooting up of the town of Columbus, New Mexico, by the renegade Mexican troops of Pancho Villa in 1916, Pershing's seniority had caught up with his rank, and President Woodrow Wilson chose him to lead the eleven thousand Regular troops that went into Mexico in pursuit of the errant Villa. The intervention failed to find its quarry, and the U.S. Government withdrew the troops early in 1917, in fair part because of the crisis with Imperial Germany over that nation's tactics of submarine warfare, tactics that took the American nation into war on April 6.

Pershing's choice as commander of the AEF was not much of a choice for the war department in Washington. Pershing had the backing, to be sure, of his father-in-law. But the choice among the half-dozen major generals of the time was fairly easy, for most of them were superannuated or ill. Only Major General Leonard Wood, who had been chief of staff during the administrations of Presidents William H. Taft and, for a few months, Wilson, amounted to a competitor, and Wood had made himself impossible by political statements and by his too close friendship with former president Roosevelt.

The reader might ask what all this has to do with the Lost Battalion, and the answer is a great deal. The AEF was to a great extent Pershing's creation. He stamped it with his personality in every way. He was the commander in chief, no doubt about it; his officers could have no doubt, for if they did not do his bidding he relieved them. His decisions, as commander in chief, were in many ways wise, and it is probably true that no other American general of his time could have done as well, but there were lapses, and sooner or later there was bound to be a Lost Battalion.

Pershing's labors in creating the AEF were beyond praise. He went off to France and presided over a small force initially of four divisions, not reinforced until the early spring of 1918. When the Russian Revolution opened the possibility that Germany would transfer masses of troops from the now-quiet eastern front to the western front, the British and French governments asked suddenly for all the American troops they could obtain. The British found shipping to help bring them over. At the same time a new U.S. Army chief of staff in Washington, General Peyton C. March, turned the army's moribund organization upside down and sent over the divisions, so that within a few months the size of the AEF increased from four to forty-two divisions, each of twenty-eight thousand men, twice and three times the size of the Allied and German divisions. Twenty-nine of those divisions were in the line during the largest and most costly battle (with twenty-six thousand deaths) in all of American history, the battle of the Meuse-Argonne, which opened on September 26, 1918, and ended with the armistice forty-seven days later, on November 11.

Pershing necessarily became one of the causes of the entrapment of the Lost Battalion because of the sheer haste with which he threw the AEF together in the spring and summer and autumn of 1918. The fact that the Lost Battalion went into the pocket was, of course, hardly Pershing's fault, directly or even indirectly. Yet the AEF was such a crash organization, if one may so describe it, that loose ends were everywhere, and that was in some part why Whittlesey and McMurtry and the men found themselves where they were on the late afternoon of October 2. It simply was not possible for Pershing or anyone to prevent some awkwardnesses, and the Lost Battalion proved awkward in the extreme as word of its plight went from every city to town to hamlet and out into the rural portions of the country, the last via newspapers carried by the postal system known as Rural Free Delivery.

Pershing was no master organizer, but his sheer forcefulness brought together within half a year an organization that was a marvel of creation, whatever the loose ends. His achievement is especially apparent if compared to the long prewar preparation of the German Army for war, so visible in that army's initial successes in August 1914; the preparation of the French Army; and the organization over many months of a large British Army in France that by 1917–1918 exceeded the size of the French Army.

The AEF's commander in chief organized the AEF on the traditional army model, with general headquarters (GHQ), First Army (not until mid-October 1918 was there a Second Army), corps, and divisions. By the end of August, First Army, which Pershing personally commanded, was ready to take part in the first all-American attack, which led to the assignment of First Army to push in a German salient fifty miles southeast of Verdun, known for its principal town of St. Mihiel. The attack opened on September 12 and ended in victory four days later.

It was here, with the taking on of St. Mihiel, that Pershing made what was probably a tactical error. For he no sooner had accepted the assignment from the Allied commander in chief, Marshal Ferdinand Foch, than Foch came back with a second request, which was to take on a larger sector to the west of Verdun, reaching from the Argonne Forest on the west to the Meuse River as it flowed from Verdun toward Sedan. The outskirts of Sedan became the top of the new American sector. Foch on August 30 went to Pershing and asked the American commander to limit the St. Mihiel battle to rolling up the salient, avoiding penetration to the north and perhaps the northeast, where a German fortress beckoned at Metz, a city whose surrounding fortification had been weakened by the withdrawal of troops to other parts of the western front.

Pershing with some calculation had accepted the St. Mihiel operation, for the AEF, now formed in part into First Army, needed to fight somewhere; this huge force could not simply continue to organize while the Allies, Britain and France—and notably the British early in August—were beginning to move forward. This state of affairs followed five great German offensives opening on March 21, 1918, which gradually petered out, one after another, the last opening on July 15 and coming to an end three days later with a Franco-American attack near Soissons.

Curiously, the American commander in chief does not seem to have used much calculation in accepting Foch's proposal to change fronts and move to the Meuse-Argonne. In not extending St. Mihiel toward Metz, he may have missed a great opportunity. At St. Mihiel he had put in his "veteran" divisions, those that had come over first and had been training through the winter of 1917–1918—that is, the First, Second, Twenty-sixth, and Forty-second divisions. Thus, he had to use green divisions to open the Meuse-Argonne battle. This required gathering nine divisions from their roles, mostly in support, at St. Mihiel and elsewhere and getting them fifty miles into the new sector—a Herculean task that involved several hundred thousands of men moving on foot or, if infantrymen and fortunate, by excruciating rides in French trucks, known as camions, that were without springs and driven by half-trained drivers, Annamites, from French Indochina. The movement of troops had to be at night to prevent the Germans from anticipating an attack in the Meuse-Argonne rather than at Metz, the logical location of a new American attack. And all this needed to be accomplished within ten days, between September 16, when it had become clear that the Germans pushed out of the St. Mihiel salient were not going to counterattack, and the opening day of the Meuse-Argonne.

Once on the new attack line, the divisions found themselves with channel-like assignments, their subsectors running north from the jump-off points. The Seventy-seventh Division received the largest of these subsector slices, seven and one-half kilometers, or five miles, wide, the upper half of the Argonne Forest. To its right, on the west bank of the meandering Aire River that flowed north, its valley bounding the heights of the Argonne until in a great sweep the river turned northwest toward the town of Grandpré, was the Twenty-eighth Division. On the left of the Seventy-seventh, at the western end of the Argonne, was the sector of the French Fourth Army, which included the U.S. Ninety-second Division, an African American outfit. The French had organized a joint Franco-American brigade under a French colonel, Groupement Durand, with which the left-hand elements of the U.S. Seventy-seventh in the forest were to keep in touch.

The second of the two dominant personalities involving the Lost Battalion, the commanding general of the Seventy-seventh Division, was Major General Alexander. What qualities did he bring to the equation on October 2–7? The answer has to be a mixture that combined with Pershing's imperious drive was bound to cause trouble.

Alexander was perhaps typical of the Regular Army men who rose to general-officer rank in World War I. He was not a graduate of West Point, which made him an exception among Pershing's senior commanders, but he had come into the army at the right time to obtain rank when the United States entered the war and the army underwent an enormous expansion, from slightly more than three hundred thousand men, counting both the Regular Army of 130,000 and the National Guard of 180,000, to four million. Alexander had enlisted in 1886, the same year Pershing graduated from the Military Academy. Pershing with his commission was a bit ahead of him, but in 1889 Alexander was commissioned. His were the ordinary experiences thereafter—that is, the Spanish-American War, in which he went to Puerto Rico, where there was almost no fighting, and then the Philippines and Mexico. Upon the declaration of war in 1917 he was a lieutenant colonel. He went to France and rose to brigadier general, and by August 27, 1918, when he took command of the Seventy-seventh, he was a major general.

Incidentally, the rank system during World War I was for promotions to take place in the so-called National Army, the name employed for drafted men. In both World Wars the army maintained a system of temporary promotions. After the armistice of November 11, 1918, many of the Regular officers lost their wartime ranks.

Some of the Regulars who rose to high rank possessed marked qualities of leadership and did well, but Alexander was not one of that select group. Something about his personality caused him to show little finesse in dealing with subordinates. In the Seventy-seventh, part of the problem may have been due to Alexander's chief of staff, Colonel J. R. R. Hannay, who transmitted orders in a blustery way. More of it was due to Alexander himself, who found sarcasm difficult to avoid. After three or four weeks with him in the Argonne, his two infantry brigadiers both asked for relief from his supervision, transferring elsewhere—anywhere, they seem to have told General Headquarters.

That Alexander did not display much diplomacy in dealing with his seniors in First Corps, First Army, or General Headquarters was another sign of his inadequacy as a senior commander, for if he had been more sensitive he would have been more careful with them, whatever he said to his infantry brigadiers. He managed to run afoul of Pershing's favorite assistant, Major General James G. Harbord, who if critical of other generals gave Alexander little benefit of any doubt, defining his abilities as not above mediocrity. This description was a Harbord favorite, and one might have written it off, but Harbord was more explicit. He said the Seventy-seventh's commander was a stuffed shirt and told Pershing's chief of staff, Major General James W. McAndrew, that when Alexander was a brigadier he was about to be relieved but instead was promoted to major general, presumably inadvertently. Harbord did say that Alexander had one redeeming quality, energy, to which, he noted, it was necessary to add "cheek," if that was a redeeming quality.[2]

Other general officers were mixed in their appraisals. Lieutenant General Robert L. Bullard, commander of Second Army, thought Alexander loud and given to talk. Bullard's counterpart, Pershing's successor as commander of First Army, Lieutenant General Hunter Liggett, thought him competent, although Liggett was known for kindly judgments, especially if they were on paper and matters of record.[3]

What made Alexander an especially awkward commander was his interaction with Pershing, who was a pusher and drew Alexander to that procedure, to a point where pushing—Pershing eventually discovered that this tactic could be a vice in management of First Army—would and could do no good.

In a very real sense the Lost Battalion's passage into the pocket came from the interaction of the two personalities, that of Pershing and that of Alexander, all of which was exacerbated by a miscalculation of Pershing's operations officers at First Army and General Headquarters. The miscalculation of the operations officers (known as G-3 in Pershing's headquarters breakdown of functions) was in undertaking the initial attack in the Meuse-Argonne on September 26 with green divisions. The Seventy-seventh had had some battle experience. So had one or two other divisions, although the experiences had been short. The rest of the divisions had spent their time in France in quiet sectors or as reserve divisions at St. Mihiel.

Pershing and his division commanders on September 26 realized that their men would have to move fast, before the German defenders recovered from the surprise that the Americans were not attacking out of the St. Mihiel front in the direction of Metz. The time in which the surprise in the Meuse-Argonne was capable of exploitation was very short, a day or two, before the Germans would bring up machine guns and emplace them in the combination of barbed wire and occasional trenches that they had planned to use for defense. The Meuse-Argonne was open warfare in most of its divisional subsectors, with the Americans moving forward and encountering, as had been the case on the rest of the western front, a series of trenches and more locked in with machine guns and artillery. But the Germans were employing new tactics—attacks by groups of machine gunners penetrating into rear areas, where they could cause chaos, and the obverse, defense by machine-gun nests supported by artillery—that had been adopted after the Battle of Riga on the eastern front in 1917, where they had proved immensely successful. Thereafter the German Army trained its attack divisions in what sometimes was described as Hutier tactics, after the victor of Riga, General Oskar von Hutier. Similarly, defense was to be elastic, gathered at places of danger to the defenders rather than fixed, as had happened in 1914–1917, in trench lines. So this was what the AEF faced on September 26, and it had to move its divisions forward rapidly before the Germans, employing interior lines, could muster enough troops for defense.

The attack on September 26 failed in a few days, because the green divisions could not get their men forward fast enough, even though on the first day most of the divisions went four or five kilometers, ordinarily a handsome gain. And in the Argonne Forest area, where the Seventy-seventh was fighting, there was a special failure, evident similarly in a few days. Here the operations plan had been to envelop the forest on both sides, with the Twenty-eighth Division surging forward along the Aire, which was on the east of the forest, and the mixed Franco-American brigade on the left moving up to secure the First Army's, and the Seventy-seventh's, left flank. There was a failure on both sides. The Twenty-eighth stalled along the heights of the Argonne, the clifflike eminences with which the forest joined the Aire valley. On the left the French and American brigade did not get far, partly because the French looked forward to American action, not their own, against the Argonne's defenders— the French Army had had enough fighting in 1914–1918 to prefer inaction, once the Americans were at hand. As for the American portion of the brigade, a regiment of the Ninety-second Division, after a few days the French Fourth Army asked for its removal from the line, and General Pershing obliged.

Pershing as First Army commander had his hands full with the attack on September 26 and then its stalling, which was thoroughly evident by October 1, so much so that the commander in chief called off the attack and reorganized for a new attack that opened on October 4 (and itself quickly stalled). When the French asked him to take out the Ninety-second he obliged, apparently without thought. He might well have put in its place one of his reserve divisions, of which he had a few. He needed something in the line on his left flank, since the French were giving the impression of attacking but retreated after German opposition, leaving a left-flank gap of at least a kilometer and more like a mile. One of the officers in the Lost Battalion who received the Congressional Medal of Honor, Captain Nelson M. Holderman of K Company, 307th Infantry, some years later wrote a paper on the Lost Battalion for the Infantry School class of 1924–1925 at Fort Benning, Georgia, in which he carefully asked why the AEF did not assign another division to replace the Ninety-second.[4] By then the issue was long since past, for the AEF did not do so, presumably because of Pershing's busyness.

It is worthwhile remarking, without any resolution to the issue, that the Ninety-second's men and officers were treated unceremoniously in their removal from the left flank, because of the French request. Despite Pershing's experience with black troops in the American West during his early years in the army, and his sobriquet of Black Jack, obtained from it, he knew disgracefully little of how to handle the African American division. In mid-August a young French nurse was shot and killed in the vicinity of the Ninety-second, and the commander in chief made it his business to drive to the headquarters of the Ninety-second, where he told the division commander, Major General Charles C. Ballou, that if another such incident occurred in the division's area he, the commander in chief, would break the division into small pieces. Word of his fury reached down to all the units, and one may only speculate on what it did for the division's morale. Pershing, of course, did not know if the individual who fired the shot was a member of the Ninety-second, but he assumed it. This may have accounted for the gingerly manner in which the Ninety-second was put into the initial attack on September 26. Under the command of Colonel Durand, only a single regiment of the Ninety-second, the 368th Infantry, went in, with its Third Battalion in attack, its First in support, and its Second in reserve. The Third withdrew twice on September 28, at noon and at 6:00 p.m., ending up at its starting point. In the AEF it was widely reported that the men had come under shell fire and scattered. In the Ninety-second's records in the National Archives there is no evidence of this (a point of interest, because many white units retreated and little was heard about that). What also was not much known was that the 368th's First Battalion under Major Charles N. Merrill, a Regular white officer (all the Ninety-second's field grade officers, majors and above, were white, save for a few medical and other nonline officers), advanced with the French to Binarville, arriving at the same time. Merrill then took his battalion forward and occupied an advance position until October 1, when his colonel sent up word that with relief of the division he had to take his men back.

What a difference it might have made in the fate of the Lost Battalion if Merrill's battalion of eight hundred men, under his tight control, had gone farther forward, and with battalions from other regiments—there were three unengaged regiments—had protected the AEF's flank, even if the lackluster French troops, an entire company of which was captured by the Germans when the latter were exploiting the gap in the lines between the Seventy-seventh Division and the French below Binarville, had failed altogether to guard the flank. The Ninety-second had sixteen thousand infantrymen, enough to keep a few hundred Germans from cutting around behind the Lost Battalion on the night of October 2–3.

An American researcher in the French archives has found records showing that the French requested the removal of the Ninety-second because of race prejudice. They did not want black troops with black company-grade officers in their command. The French custom was to provide white officers and noncommissioned officers for colonial troops.[5] After the war Major Merrill met Colonel Durand during the occupation of the Rhineland, and Durand corroborated that it was for this reason that the French Fourth Army high command wanted the Ninety-second Division out of the line.[6]

A sign of what was in store for the Lost Battalion came on September 28 when Major Whittlesey with the First Battalion of the 308th Infantry encamped at a place known as Moulin de l'Homme Mort (Dead Man's Mill), to the south of what was to become the pocket of October 2–7. Whittlesey found his battalion surrounded. He had put his four companies in a square perimeter and established runner posts back to the regimental commander. The battalion was at the left end of the Seventy-seventh's subsector, the last American troops other than Merrill's battalion, which was too far to the west to be of assistance. The tactical picture as it developed that night and the next day, until relief came, was not pretty. Lieutenant Colonel Fred E. Smith took a small detachment and passed his men up a path that he thought led to Whittlesey's battalion. Instead he ran into German machine guns. The colonel drew his pistol and opened fire while his men took cover. Not only was his place exposed, but he was also wounded in the side. Giving no attention to his injury, he made his way to a hand grenade dump, under enemy fire, and returned for the purpose of another attack on the enemy emplacements. As he was attempting to ascertain the exact location of the nearest nest he fell, mortally wounded. He was awarded the Congressional Medal posthumously.

Whittlesey and his men were relieved on September 30 and were ready for what proved a new, and for them all nearly fatal, attack that opened for the 308th Regiment at 12:50 p.m., October 2.

two   October 2–3

In the decision to send six companies from two battalions of the 308th up a large ravine for a kilometer into German-held territory on October 2, responsibility lay primarily with Generals Pershing and Alexander.

The AEF's commander in chief was no more than formally responsible, for he was supervising the entire battle of the Meuse-Argonne, of which the maneuvers of a battalion or two hardly counted. But it was the élan, to employ the French word so often heard in 1917–1918, that Pershing displayed to his commanders that led them onward, encouraging them to push their troops through to victory in a way that, given the green divisions in the Meuse-Argonne, was not easily possible. The pushing was too hard, considering the training of the men, and necessitated calling a halt to the initial attack of September 26. Pershing would resume the attack on October 4. There would be another resumption on October 14. After that he brought in the commander of First Corps, General Liggett, who called a two-week halt to offensive operations and reorganized First Army for what proved, when it opened November 1, to be the final attack of the AEF, marvelously successful, preceded by a masterful artillery preparation and barrage that rolled up the German defenders in a retreat across the Meuse and beyond, ending with the armistice.

Pershing was no tactician. His principal quality was resolution, and this he installed in his division commanders. He would relieve a major general in a flash if he considered the man irresolute. In this regard the word was out, and his generals were fearful of him. In organizing the AEF, and accomplishing the task in six months, the commander in chief's imperiousness, his desire for generals who would take their men forward, had much to say for it, but when the divisions were in the field this quality was not altogether helpful.

As an observer could have predicted, with the failure of the initial attack Pershing was sure the cause was the faltering of commanders. In the center of the line, in Fifth Corps, the Seventy-ninth Division failed to take the height of Montfaucon on the first day—it took it on the second—and, Pershing believed, held up the entire line. He learned that the division on the Seventy-ninth's right flank, the Fourth in the neighboring Third Corps, could have shoved troops up above Montfaucon and threatened the height from the rear, but instead the chief of staff of Third Corps, a brigadier general, insisted that corps and division boundaries should govern. The leading brigade in the Fourth Division, eight thousand men, reached the corps goal by 1:00 p.m. and stopped there for the rest of the day; the support brigade, another eight thousand rifles, stayed in place behind it. The moment was lost.

With the failure of the initial attack, Pershing thus was sure that more attacks, an accumulation, would win out, and he let it be known—his division commanders had known this before—that he wanted forward action from everyone. In the Argonne Forest this meant the Seventy-seventh Division, and General Alexander knew that he did not need to wait for the AEF attack scheduled for October 4. He had nearly the entire forest to himself, and the need was for the men to go forward.

Alexander knew that too much attention to flanks had been the undoing of First Army before and to the right of Montfaucon, and he was himself temperamentally disposed to attack. He gave little attention to his division's flank with the French Fourth Army. In telling Whittlesey's brigade commander, Brigadier General Evan M. Johnson, to send companies forward into what would prove to be a pocket, he gave Johnson assurance that the French would come up or had come up. Johnson later said he was uneasy about his flank, but it was difficult at the moment to deny Alexander's assurance. Alexander did not know where the French were, only that General Pershing wanted all the divisions to move ahead and that this meant his, the Seventy-seventh.

1

That first day, Wednesday, October 2, saw the men of the attack battalion, Whittlesey's, and of the support battalion, McMurtry's, each with three companies rather than the table-of-organization four, move up to the Charlevaux Brook and the north side of the valley through which the brook flowed. That side, although they had no way of knowing it, was to become the pocket.

The advance of Whittlesey's force on October 2 marked the only forward advance on the entire front of First Army from the Argonne Forest to the Meuse. The rest of First Army would resume the attack later.

The Seventy-seventh attacked along its seven-and-one-half-kilometer front, with the 153rd Infantry Brigade on the right, next to the Twenty-eighth Division in the Aire valley. The brigade was seeking to move up to a German strong point by the name of Le Chêne Tondu, which had stopped the Twenty-eighth because of its dominance of the river valley. Under Brigadier General Edmund C. Wittenmyer the brigade went forward for a while but stopped at the strong point, unable to proceed any farther. The 153rd Brigade of the Seventy-seventh, incidentally, conducted its operations separately from those of the 154th under General Johnson, to the left, and so far as concerned the 308th Regiment on the far left, and for that matter its sister regiment the 307th, had little to do with the 154th's successes or failures. One of the disadvantages of the Seventy-seventh Division's wide sector was this separation of the infantry brigades, a virtual separation of its operations which proved to be a disconcerting factor in General Alexander's calculations, for he was forever turning his attention from one brigade to the other, right to left and back again.

The 154th under Johnson sent its 307th Regiment forward to the right of the 308th, and it enjoyed some slight success before running into the usual German cordon of twenty or thirty yards of barbed wire and behind it sited machine guns. These were the defenses of what the Germans described as the Giselher Stellung, the first of three successive positions in the Hindenburg Line that ran all the way across the front of First Army. The positions were named after Wagnerian witches—Giselher, Kriemhilde, and Freya, the last far up to the north in the hills of Buzancy and not completed. The most important was the Kriemhilde Stellung, not yet encountered by the Seventy-seventh.

General Alexander gave out his instructions to Johnson, who passed them to the 308th's new commander, Colonel Cromwell Stacey, who gave them to the commander of the regiment's attack battalion, Whittlesey. The object was to be gained without regard to losses, he said. As to the 308th's flank with the French to the left, he does not seem to have been clear.[1] He told the assistant inspector of the First Army, Captain Albert T. Rich, in an interrogation of October 7, that he knew the flank was open. At this time Whittlesey's force was still in the pocket, its fate not known—there was in fact uncertainty as to whether the Lost Battalion was still fighting. General Johnson, also interrogated, told Rich that Alexander assured him that the French were ahead of the 308th.[2] It was confusing. Alexander and Johnson perhaps were already preparing their defenses.

To give a push to his order to the commander of the 154th Brigade, Alexander told Johnson over the field telephone that if he, Johnson, could not manage an attack as Alexander stipulated, the division commander would get someone who could.

The attack began as ordered. It was preceded by an artillery barrage, advancing ahead of the troops. Captain Holderman of K Company in his Fort Benning paper wrote that the barrage was for morale rather than material result. Men felt better when they heard artillery firing ahead. The commander of the division's artillery, Brigadier General Manus McCloskey, like Alexander, must have been confused by the wide division front, almost the length of the range of his two regiments of light artillery, which were firing French 75s. His guns, back in division line, could not reach far. He would have been firing blind, by the map, from a map that showed only a trackless forest. He knew a German strong point or two and could fire at it or them, but for the rest of them he was limited to digging holes or spreading shrapnel indiscriminately, in ravines, trees, and bushes in front of the 308th Infantry.

Whittlesey took forward companies A, B, C, E, G, and H. The size of the companies varied, and no one knew exactly how many men were in each. The table of organization for AEF divisions called for two hundred and fifty men in an infantry company. None of Whittlesey's companies approached that size. According to approximate figures collected in France in April 1919, the companies of what would become the Lost Battalion varied widely: A, 18; B, 54; C, 85; E, 21; G, 56; H, 101. In addition there were headquarters, runners, and scouts of the First and Second battalions, 65 men; two sections of the 306th Machine Gun Battalion, 53 men; and 3 first-aid men. The total was 456.[3] Alexander wrote afterward that he thought Whittlesey's companies were down to forty men each, a surprising guess on Alexander's part, for it showed him without any clear notion of company strength in the 308th.[4]

A day or two before the battalions attacked, the 154th Brigade received, and it is possible that they were counted in the returns of the 308th Regiment, twenty-one hundred new men who were parceled to the various companies. The new men were without training, many not having fired a rifle—which produced stories of men who did not know what end of the Springfield to put the bullets in. The men were from the Forty-first Division, a depot division, meaning it had been turned into replacements. Evidently the new men received no training while they waited to learn where they were going. None had seen a grenade. They could do little more than close-order drill and would bunch if in any action. Practically speaking, they could be used only as carriers and for behind-the-line tasks. In the event they soon found themselves in the line, many of them wounded or killed.

The goal was the Charlevaux valley, a kilometer beyond the starting point. Fortunately the south-to-north ravine up which the men passed was wide. In fact, it was a huge ravine. Captain McMurtry estimated it at six to eight hundred yards, perhaps half a mile, across. The men went up on the east side. Two companies led out, with the scouts in front. The men crept along in platoon columns. Behind the advance companies were two companies in support. Behind them was a composite company, men from Companies A and G, which McMurtry at Whittlesey's orders had combined before the men went forward, the companies having been reduced because of casualties. As the men slowly moved forward Whittlesey dropped off runner posts every two hundred yards. These were so-called cossack posts, of two or more men each.

The two battalions cautiously advanced, capturing a few Germans, two officers and twenty-eight men, with three machine guns. This small force did not bother to fire its guns, whether seeing the size of the American force or demoralized. As the Americans were to discover, they were up against adversaries in their thirties, forties, even fifties—some were of the Landwehr (garrison) troops, and others were of the 254th Regiment, Seventy-sixth Reserve Division, similarly overage. They were troops of experience, some of whom had spent two and one-half months on the Soissons front. Their companies were depleted. A prisoner taken on October 3 told Whittlesey that the companies were down to seventy men.

The advance up the side of the broad ravine was not without opposition, and the casualties of Whittlesey's force should have been alarming, although with General Alexander's injunction to advance without regard to losses they apparently seemed all right. During the almost five hours that the men moved forward, from 12:50 until around 5:30, the column sustained eight men killed and eighty wounded. These deaths and injuries were from sniper fire, seemingly from the west, or left, side of the ravine, where scouts and troops occasionally were too visible.

There was attention to the ravine's west side. Two companies of the 308th, one from each of the battalions, were put in there. They did not move forward as rapidly as did the men on the east side and proved of no value in keeping down snipers.

Speaking of the left flank, it was not until four days after Whittlesey started out, that is, until October 6, the day before the Lost Battalion was relieved, that the Seventy-seventh Division's situation on its left flank become clear. On that date the division G-3, the assistant chief of staff for operations, Lieutenant Colonel M. W. Howze, gave Alexander a memorandum about what had happened on the flank in terms of liaison, by which he meant how forces on the left had kept up, or not kept up, with the Seventy-seventh. The French had attacked on October 2, as they said they would, and reached a German strong point, La Palette Pavillon, below Charlevaux Mill; the mill was near where the 308th companies were heading. There the German defenders proved more valiant than the French, who retreated back to Binarville. No French attacks occurred thereafter. On the afternoon of October 4, Howze discussed the matter with Alexander and suggested that the general's French aide go to the commanding general of the French forces and ask him to move forward. The aide returned with word that the French would move the next morning. During the night it was learned that the French attack on October 5 had been called off.

Back on October 2, Whittlesey's command halted when he and

McMurtry and the men arrived at the top of Hill 198. In front lay a broad valley, that of Charlevaux. The north slope of the valley was visible, with their objective as set out in their instructions, which was the Charlevaux Mill and the Binarville-Apremont road. The commanders gazing across the valley could dimly see the road running east-west. The mill lay four hundred yards from their view of the road, to the west.

The prospect was attractive. A steep quarrylike edge had been cut into the slope to the north of the road, and above the edge the hill rose sharply to the crest. Here, they decided, was a place in which the men could halt for the night, while reinforcements were coming up. It appeared to be easily defensible.

What happened is best put in the words of a chapter for a history of the 308th Regiment published by one of its officers, Captain L. Wardlaw Miles, in 1927:

> As soon as the disposition by companies was decided upon, the word to advance was given and the command, including the machine gunners, filed down the slope, through the morass at the bottom of the ravine, and crossed the diminutive Charlevaux brook on a narrow plank bridge. As they crossed the brook, the men noticed that the view along the valley was open to the right and to the left of them. They took up a position just below the road covering ground 300 yards long and 60 yards deep. The slope was found to be steep, thickly wooded, and covered with underbrush. It was supposed that this position on a reverse slope would offer protection against hostile artillery fire. Although the hard and rocky ground opposed stiff resistance to entrenching tools wielded by tired arms, the command dug itself in for the night within an hour. The plan of disposition marked an oblong formation, its long sides running parallel with the southern edge of the Charlevaux [Binarville-Apremont] road.[5]

As to how the companies of the 308th ended up in what became a pocket, two questions remain concerning the events of Wednesday, October 2.

One was the possibility, raised after the war by a newspaperman, Thomas M. Johnson, that the 308th missed a great opportunity by passing into the pocket and spending what proved a quiet, uneventful night asleep among the dense trees and bushes. Johnson's judgment was worth attention, for in 1938 he joined with a military writer, Fletcher Pratt, to produce what, for its time, was the definitive book on the Lost Battalion. Johnson knew a good deal and was present on October 8 when half of the remaining men of Whittlesey's command, led by their major, walked out of the pocket, disheveled and yet glad to be relieved, and moved back to a point where they could gain transport to hospitals and holding areas and rest from their ordeal.[6]

Johnson believed that the French and the division could have made an advance on both sides of Whittlesey's force—if the troops on the left, the French soldiers seeking to take La Palette Pavillon, and those on the right, the 307th, had managed together with the Lost Battalion to advance upon the German defenders. There was something to be said for this. The French may well not have put their best effort into the La Palette attack. On the right a company of the 307th had wandered through a gap in the German wire and was on the east side of the Charlevaux valley, where it might have linked with Whittlesey. According to German testimony after the war, the defending force was fearful it would have to withdraw. The appearance of the French at La Palette was threatening, and with Whittlesey's force coming up the ravine, and unknown forces behind it, the few defenders typified by Whittlesey's capture of the thirty men and officers of a machine-gun unit and by the otherwise lack of opposition were cut in two by the oncoming Americans. Pressure on their flanks might have driven them back to the Kriemhilde Stellung, forcing them to give up the Giselher Stellung.

Lieutenant General Richard Wellmann, who commanded the German First Reserve Corps, wrote that Whittlesey deserved credit for driving north but was timid when he passed his men into the pocket.[7] What would have been necessary was, unfortunately, much more, and much better, liaison with the French, who if close to the Americans were not all that close and seem to have known nothing of Whittlesey's advance. On the right flank, as the 307th's company moved into the valley, it too was ignorant that an American force was to its left, and so its commander, understandably concerned about being outflanked, took his men back through the gap in the wire through which they had come, rejoining his regiment.

Whittlesey by Wellmann's measure was timid. But the major had said to McMurtry and others when on Hill 198, "Our objective is the other side of the valley, not this side." He stopped below the Binarville-Apremont road because those was his orders. Given the uncertainties of his flanks, and the certainties of his orders, what else was he to do?

The other question that arose after the war concerned Whittlesey's and McMurtry's judgment in putting their men in a pocket on the reverse slope of the hill beyond Hill 198, on the north side of the Charlevaux valley. Apart from his orders, Whittlesey easily could see that being on a reverse slope protected him and his men from hostile artillery, the trajectories of the shells of which would fall on whatever Germans stationed themselves on Hill 198, the valley's south slope. On the morning of Thursday, October 3, German artillery to the northeast tried to shell the Americans and for the most part failed. If the Lost Battalion had put men on the crest of their side of the ravine, above the road, they would have invited further artillery fire.

As for trying to hold the ground from the crest to the road, that was hardly necessary because of the steepness of the bank and especially the manner in which the road cut into the bank, for attackers had to jump on the road while coming down. There was not much cover, either, for seventy-five yards—quite a distance. Thus, any attackers coming down would be exposing themselves to rifle fire.

Below the American line, into the valley through which ran Charlevaux Brook and up on the other side to the crest of Hill 198, was a barren area, two hundred yards in width. It was only necessary to hold the Lost Battalion's south border lightly, for troops trying to cross such a distance were asking for trouble. The flanks, east and west, were covered by Hotchkiss guns, two on each side, fifteen yards apart. Not without reason did the Germans describe the American position as the *Amerikanernest.*

A U.S. Army special forces lieutenant colonel, Taylor V. Beattie, who for years has made a habit of visiting the pocket of the Lost Battalion—walking over the area down to the brook, which he finds has been altered into pools, walking on to the crest of Hill 198, and from there viewing the scene of the Lost Battalion's travail—recently has offered a particular objection to Whittlesey's dispositions on the reverse slope. Beattie argues that Whittlesey was a citizen soldier, as were most of the officers in the AEF (the Regular Army mustered 5,769 officers on April 1, 1917, and needed 200,000). This meant, the colonel wrote, that the major was indifferently trained in tactics and therefore made the mistake of a junior officer, putting his men in a pocket that was too deep for easy defense, because the men would have found themselves caught in their own fields of fire. He sees no reason for having a depth of nearly two hundred feet.[8]

Colonel Beattie's point sounds unexceptionable but overlooks two factors in defense of the pocket. One was that the men after the first night, finding themselves harassed by sniper and machine-gun and mortar fire, needed to stay in their funkholes (the World War I name for foxholes) unless there was a general attack from the front, the rear, or the sides. Then they climbed out of the holes, took stations at distances not far from them, and were ready for the enemy. It was not a matter of firing from the holes.

The other reason for the depth of the pocket was the numbers of wounded. Eighty men had been wounded simply in passing the companies up the ravine into the pocket. Some of them must have been lightly wounded and capable of taking part in the defense. Others, surely, were incapable—or, as time told, able only to reload rifles for their comrades. The seriously wounded (their numbers increased rapidly as the days passed, but already Whittlesey had his hands full with them) had to be put somewhere, and the reasonable place was in funkholes in the middle of the pocket.

Upon placing the men in the pocket, Whittlesey put a patrol on the crest of the hill in front and posted guards at the flanks. After the men had dug their funkholes they broke out and shared what food was available, so-called iron rations, meaning two-pound cans of "bully beef" and hardtack crackers. The force was not fully provided with rations. The division's G-4 organization, the supply officers and men, had brought up rations just prior to the companies' going forward, but some men did not get them. McMurtry was so busy attempting to join Companies A and G that he obtained no rations.[9] After the meal, of what was available, the men turned in, and the night was very quiet.

The major and the men had reason to believe that they had done well. They had broken the German *Hauptwiderstandslinie,* the line of the Giselher Stellung. They had arrived where General Alexander told them to go.

The authors Johnson and Pratt concluded that General Johnson, the brigade commander, had reason to heave a sigh of relief. Hectored by Alexander, told that the division commander would relieve him, he could contemplate that the 307th Regiment under Lieutenant Colonel Eugene H. Houghton had made no progress, but that was in early reports, and presumably they had done all right later. And a message had come back through Whittlesey's runner chain that the 308th had broken through the German trench line, at a place where the trenches ran across on both sides of the ravine but the Germans had failed to wire the area between. At that place no German troops were in sight and the 308th went through.

2

Thursday, October 3, the first full day that the Lost Battalion spent in the pocket, turned out to be a strange experience. Whittlesey knew the men had been surrounded. That became evident by early afternoon. Later the enemy made two sharp attacks. Yet throughout that day, and for the next day, Friday, October 4, none of the men thought for a moment that the experience would differ much from what the 308th had gone through with four companies in the Moulin de l'Homme Mort pocket from September 28 to 30. Pockets, it seemed, were inevitable within the Argonne Forest, where liaison was so difficult.

The day opened with an encouraging event, the appearance of Holderman with K Company of the 307th. With ninety-eight men, K was one of the more sizable companies within the Seventy-seventh Division. The preceding afternoon General Alexander, anticipating trouble, had asked General Johnson to send up reinforcements and use the division reserve, the Third Battalion, 307th, and Johnson sent up Companies I, K, L, and M. K first, followed by M, L, and I, in that order. They were in single file, with Holderman and his second in command, First Lieutenant Thomas G. Pool, out in front. Holderman had not felt well that day but refused to leave his men, telling Pool that if he dropped out it would appear as if he had abandoned his men, and he would rather die on the field than give such an impression.

On the way something strange happened, which perhaps was not unusual for troops in action where rumors started and could cause problems. Word passed up to Holderman and Pool to about-face, that the order sending reinforcements had been revoked. Pool went back, as fast as he could, telling each of the men to stop in place, to discover that M Company already had turned back and was gone, impossible to hunt for. Similarly L and I companies had turned. Whoever passed up this order must have been in I Company. The lieutenant went up again to the front, and Holderman and he passed the word back that under no circumstances should the men obey an order from the rear. With this they went on and, upon the approach of darkness, which came early in the Meuse-Argonne, for this was October, bivouacked three hundred meters south of Whittlesey's position, before joining the battalions of the 308th early the following morning, at 6:30.

At daybreak, 6:00, on October 3, Whittlesey ordered Lieutenant Karl Wilhelm, commanding E Company, to go back along the west side of the ravine and see if they could find and bring up the two companies of the 308th, D and F, under Lieutenant Paul Knight, that had been put on that side at the outset of the advance. Whittlesey had wanted to do this the night before, but dusk had approached and his men were tired; thus, he waited until morning. He presumed some Germans might have gotten in between the companies and his own position but calculated that E Company could drive them out and bring the companies up. There was no runner chain on the west side, and perhaps they needed direction.

Wilhelm got into a hot action, and E Company scattered. Just how many men were in the company is debatable, probably fifty or sixty, the equivalent of a platoon under full complement. Germans were everywhere, firing into Wilhelm's ranks, and he told Lieutenant James V. Leak to get out as many men he could and go back to the men in the pocket. Leak came in with two squads, eighteen men. Most of Wilhelm's company was captured, with the captain and four men managing to get through to 308th regimental headquarters.

When Holderman and K Company came in, Whittlesey placed them on the right of the pocket, behind the two Hotchkiss guns (with a Chauchat gunner at the top of the crest above the Binarville-Apremont road to warn in case of attack before retiring back to the Hotchkiss guns). At 8:00 a.m. Whittlesey sent for Holderman and ordered him to take his company south across Charlevaux Brook and up Hill 198, to determine whether he could get back to the Seventy-seventh from that direction, the east side of the ravine.

Holderman ran into the same problem Wilhelm had: large numbers of Germans. As he started out he heard a voice shouting across the valley that he and the men were coming. He heard a guttural response on the other side. With this he moved the company in gingerly fashion. There was a small road at the foot of the hill, which the Germans had enfiladed with machine guns on the left flank and snipers on the road. There seemed to be snipers in the rear. Taking the men across the road was difficult, and after the warning across the valley Holderman waited an hour. About 1:00 he managed to get the company across by filtering a few at a time, with what he believed were three casualties, not many under the circumstances. The company established a position on the hill, and he sent patrols to feel for enemy troops—he had encountered no more. The patrols reported no enemy; they could see none. At that point the men were two hundred yards out from their starting place in the pocket.

K Company sent forward three patrols penetrating due south, with scouts well out and strong combat groups covering the flanks. They passed through an initial system of barbed wire and then came under galling flank and frontal machine-gun and rifle fire. They continued, firing as they advanced, into a second barbed wire system.

It became evident that a powerful force had surrounded them and withdrawal was necessary. How many Germans Holderman confronted is difficult to say. After the war a German officer said that during the night his regiment worked one hundred and eighty men between the Americans in the pocket and the main force to the rear. After a hard fight, Holderman recalled, he managed to withdraw the company back to the position occupied by Whittlesey's men. Carrying its wounded, K Company arrived at 1:30 p.m., with a rear guard of thirty men holding off the enemy.

After Holderman's return, Whittlesey and McMurtry talked things over and passed to the officers the following word: "Our mission is to hold this position at all costs. No falling back. Have this understood by every man in your command."

During the morning it became evident that the Germans behind the Lost Battalion had broken the runner posts. How Whittlesey learned this is hard to say, but in his after-action report of October 9 he said he had learned at 10:30 that two posts had been dispersed. Apparently the Germans left the chain until last, meanwhile taking measures against Wilhelm on the left and Holderman on the right. In his Fort Benning paper Holderman stated that he believed this was a ruse, cutting off the flank movements first.

By this time the sole enemy shelling of the position had taken place, not very successfully. At 8:00 a.m. a German airplane flew over, and a half hour later the shelling commenced, an enfilade—that is, a flank fire—from the northwest, for it was impossible to strike the American force from the north because of its reverse slope position. This led to the first pigeon message, released at 8:50: "We are being shelled by German artillery. Can we have artillery support? Fire is coming from northwest."[10] American artillery soon found the enemy batteries and forced them out.

More important, the Germans brought up a heavy trench mortar and suddenly opened fire from a position six hundred yards to the northwest. The mortar fired on the American position twice a day for an hour each time. The shells did go into the American position, but most of them proved to be duds. It was estimated that 10 to 15 percent of the mortar shells—which continued until American artillery took the mortar out on October 5—were effective. Scouts found the vicinity of the mortar, and a squad went to get it, but a machine gun protected it, and they could not get close enough. The men in the pocket had to put up with it.

All of which prompted Holderman in his paper to a suggestion that approximated a criticism of his senior commanders, Stacey, Johnson, perhaps Alexander. Holderman had to be careful with Alexander, who wrote an enthusiastic letter of endorsement that Holderman appended to the front of his Benning essay. The paper required proposals, and the captain's second one was, "Never allow a force as large as a battalion to start on any mission without supporting weapons, in the form of the 37 millimeter guns, trench mortars and machine guns."[11] The Lost Battalion had taken the last, but not the others. This was typical of attack units during the early days of the Meuse-Argonne, for many went in without the small 37-millimeter one-pounder cannons and Stokes mortars. The problem was bringing them up, for they were heavy and required carts. Over tangled or ravine-dominated terrain, carts were difficult.

The failure of Wilhelm's company, the artillery and mortar attacks, the opening of machine-gun fire from the left flank principally, also across the valley, and the increasing sniper fire led

Whittlesey to release his second pigeon message at 10:45, which arrived in a French loft at Colombey at 11:35 and was received at division headquarters message center at 12:10.

> Our runner posts are broken. One runner captured. Germans in small numbers are working in our left rear about 294.6–276.2. Have sent K Company 307th to occupy this hill [Hill 198] and open the line.
>
> Patrol to east ran into Germans at 295.1–276.3. (6 Boches).
>
> Have located German mortar at 294.05–276.30 and have sent platoon to get it.
>
> Have taken prisoner who says his company of seventy men were brought in here last night 294.4–276.2 from rear by motor trucks. He saw only a few infantrymen here when he came in. German machine gun constantly firing on valley in our rear from hill 294.1–276.0. E Company (sent to meet D and F) met heavy resistance, at least twenty casualties. Two squads under Lieutenant Leak have just fallen back here.
>
> > Whittlesey
> > Major, 308th Inf.

All the above, beginning at daylight with the sending out of E Company under Wilhelm, was preliminary to two attacks the Germans made that afternoon, at 3:00 and 5:00. Once or twice a day, from then onward, came the attacks: the two above-mentioned on October 3, two the next day, one each on October 5 and 6, and two on October 7, for a total of eight attacks in five days.

The first attack on October 3 was a surprise affair, made with the view of storming the position. The main attack was from the front, from the crest of the reverse slope that dropped to the road, the latter cut into the side of the hill and requiring jumping. All this was largely in the open, including of course the road. The German plan was for grenadiers to carry "potato mashers," hurling the grenades and moving down the cliff during the explosions.

It was fortunate that the Lost Battalion's men had taken extra ammunition when they moved out, having anticipated trouble. It was also fortunate that the American troops, or at least those that had been trained, were good shots with their rifles, compared to the French and British, who trusted more to fusillades than to deliberate aim. The German line came down together, sending barrages and scuttling forward during bursts. There were three barrages. At the start of the fourth the enemy was close enough for its line to be visible. A rippling fire went up to the line, each shot aimed. As the newspaperman Johnson and the historian Pratt described it, "There was a choir of shrieks; half a dozen bombs burst at the feet of the men who had meant to throw them as they collapsed under that surprise shooting. Somebody on our side began to yell. 'Shut up!' The attack stopped."[12]

The 3:00 attack led to the third pigeon message, released at 4:05, arriving at 4:25, telephoned to the Seventy-seventh message center at 4:55:

> Germans are on cliff north of us in small numbers and have tried to envelop both flanks. Situation on left flank very serious.
> Broke two of our runner posts today near 294.7–275.7. We have not been able to reestablish posts today.
> Need 8,000 rounds rifle ammunition 7,500 Chauchat, 23 boxes M.G. and 250 offensive grenades.
> Casualties yesterday in companies here (A, B, C, E, G, H), 8 killed, 80 wounded. In same companies today, 1 killed 60 wounded.
> Present effective strength of companies here, 245. Situation serious.
>
> Whittlesey

Falling back, the enemy began planning another attack. Too eager, the Germans gave away their plan. An American officer on the left of the pocket who understood and spoke German overheard the officers talking back and forth, calling to each other, giving instructions.

"Rudolph," a guttural voice would call.

"Hier," the answer came from the bushes above the outposts on the extreme left.

"Heinrich," the same voice called.

"Ich bin hier," was the answer.

There were more commands in German and then, after a final shout of "Nun, alle zusammen," the attack started.[13]

The attack came off at 5:00, a fierce affair as Holderman remembered it. The enemy attacked both flanks, simultaneously, with infantry groups. The grenadiers on the crest in front supported them. The big mortar to the northwest opened. Machine-gun fire raked the flanks and came in from Hill 198 across the valley. Again the Americans waited—almost like their ancestors at Bunker Hill—until the enemy was in full view. Then, when they heard the command to fire, "the ravine rang out with echoes of machine guns, Chauchat rifles, and rifles." The American machine gunners swept the hill on the other side. "The men were steady, cool, and deliberate during the delivery of their fire."[14] General Pershing, well known for his advice to men of the AEF to be sure to know how to manage rifle fire, certain that such fire would carry them through machine-gun nests, even artillery fire, had he been present, would have been proud of the Lost Battalion as it fired that afternoon.

Again the Germans fell back. Cries of pain were heard everywhere. They continued until darkness, when it was possible for the Germans to come forward and pick up their dead and wounded. This the enemy did every night during the days the Americans were in the pocket. Except it was impossible to retrieve the dead close to the American lines; the Americans then had the task of burying those bodies, which they did until the next day, October 4, when weakness from hunger and exhaustion from repelling attacks made it impossible.

The night of October 3–4, like the first night, passed quietly. There were a few shells from American 75s far to the rear, but no hostile action.

As on the previous night, the mood of the Americans that night and into the next day was positive. They felt that the main body of the division, which during the day could be heard firing to the south behind them, would come up and, as had happened on September 30, relieve them.

three   October 4–5

By Friday, October 4, the condition of Whittlesey's men was turn-ing serious. Upon arrival everything had been all right. On Wednes-day the pocket seemed the place for a bivouac, after which, they assumed by the next morning or so, the line of the 154th Brigade would straighten out, with the 307th Regiment under Colonel Hough-ton coming up even with Whittlesey's position. On the left the French, too, would be up. The German defenders seemed to be no large group and presumably would be gone, on their way north prob-ably to the bend of the Aire below Grandpré. The next day, Thurs-day, October 3, likewise seemed basically all right, even though the men were surrounded; this had happened before at Moulin l'Homme Mort. But by Friday, for the men who were still in the pocket (at Moulin de l'Homme Mort they had only been in two days), the pros-pect was not so good.

That morning of October 4, an hour and a half after daybreak, at 7:25, Whittlesey sent out the fourth message by his air service. As was his wont he gave the force's coordinates.

> All quiet during the night. Our patrols indicate Germans with-drew during the night. Sending further patrols now to verify this report. At 12:30 and 1:10 a.m. six shells from our own light ar-tillery fell on us. Many wounded here whom we can't evacuate. Need rations badly. No word from D or F companies.
>
> Whittlesey
> Major, 308th Inf.

1

Whittlesey's fourth message offers a good indication of how matters would progress on October 4, and for that matter over the weekend—the long weekend as it turned out, until Monday evening and the sound, or so it seemed, of the pipes at Lucknow.

Whittlesey mentioned no Germans and presumed their withdrawal, but of course he was mistaken. Every morning the major sent out patrols, probably sound military doctrine in combat. The patrols saw Germans in the forest and knew that more were nearby, all around. However, the patrols proved, over the days of the siege, to be terribly costly, for men would be hit by snipers or bursts of machine-gun fire, and their comrades had to bring them back.

The patrols returned with wounded, whose plight was of increasing concern. In the funkholes in the middle of the pocket they were safe, provided they did not stir too much or, if under machine-gun fire, raise their heads. During the machine-gun fusillades that came over principally from the left flank, the wounded had to stay flat. The heavy mortar, impossible to take out because of its machine gun, was throwing projectiles twice a day, and while most of them went into the bottom of the valley and those landing in the pocket were more often than not duds, there were just enough hits to keep wounded heads down.

The force had no physician and only three first-aid men, who did the best they could with what medical supplies they had at hand. The number of first-aid men was minuscule, considering the number of wounded. Too, by the end of Thursday, October 3, bandages had run out. The men had first-aid kits, which were pooled, and the first-aid men carried bandages, but there were not nearly enough. Soon the first-aid men were taking bandages from the dead, nauseous strips that were blood-stained and stiff, better not seen by the newly wounded, with the sole advantage of allowing wounds to be bound in order to stop the flow of blood. For bandaging wounds the first-aid men also resorted to a novelty that worked, one that probably never had been thought of when the army's quartermaster department designed the uniforms for the troops. While the officers, as befitted their rank, had received boots, the men had wrap-around pieces that started at their feet and spiraled up over their trousers. These wrap-arounds looked neat; they kept dust, dirt, sand, pebbles, and other debris from going up trouser legs; and presumably they added to morale.[1] They could be washed, when washing was possible. The first-aid men began using the wrap-arounds, taking them off the dead, and then off the living. Woolen, they soaked up blood like gauze bandages. The strips were strong and could be pulled tightly around stubs of arms or legs or lacerated wounds—hoping the material was clean enough not to cause infections.

Beginning on Friday, October 4, it was impossible to bury the dead, whether the German bodies around the periphery of the pocket or, of more concern, the American ones within. The men were too tired. The ground in the pocket was hard to dig in, and space was running out, there being little between the trees or under bushes with frequently deep roots. In an unchivalrous act the Germans directed trench mortar, machine-gun, and rifle fire at burial parties. There was a morale problem in leaving bodies aboveground, even if men covered the heads of the unfortunates. The year 1918 was still the time of funereal America; funerals were solemn matters, and burial seemed a necessity. In describing what happened when bodies could not be buried, Holderman was obviously touched. He wrote not merely of a melancholy duty but of a "last earthly tribute."[2] The morale problem was complicated by what might be described as the smell problem, for the unburied made their presence known. When the relief force, the 307th Regiment, began its final approach to their comrades, early on the evening of October 7, the smell of the dead told them where the pocket lay.

Lack of food constantly affected the men. Whittlesey's message early that morning said "need rations badly," which was an understatement, as the men had eaten their iron rations during the move up the ravine and consumed the last of their food the next noon. Hunger thereupon set in. Survivors all mentioned that the worst of the hunger was at the outset. Perhaps this was akin to the hunger that individuals feel when they pass up meals; there was something psychic about it. It subsided, giving way to a dull emptiness that became so customary it seemed natural. One way to allay it, through the five days beginning October 3, was to drink water.

Obtaining water was a problem. When the men came in to the position they walked down Hill 198 and crossed on the wooden footbridge. At the bottom, surrounded by marsh, was the brook. This water was muddy, but if it stood in a canteen the mud settled. The real problem was getting it, which was possible only at night. In daytime snipers covered the brook. Machine guns on the left flank could fire down. During nighttime the machine gunners fired bursts in knowledge that they might catch men on water detail. In the daytime it was tempting for men in the pocket to drift down toward the brook and try to fill canteens, and after a few were wounded Whittlesey put in a water guard during the day; the last thing the force needed was more wounded.

The pigeon message mentioned the failure of D and F Companies to come up. These were the companies that Wilhelm with E Company had gone back to get but was prevented from reaching when the Germans surrounded his own company.

Fortunately, the weather cooperated fairly well during the stay of Whittlesey's men on the reverse slope. When they went into the forest on September 26, the Argonne, indeed the entire American sector to the Meuse, proved no place for good weather. Just before the attack on September 26 the men had enjoyed the beautiful autumnal weather, what at home they would have described as Indian summer. Trees were turning brown and gold, and because of the quiet during the day, since the men were moving forward at night, it was possible to believe they were home enjoying the last of the fall season. The first day of the general attack had been a golden day and remained in memory as that, despite the din that accompanied their movement. But then, on September 27, the weather changed, as they might have expected, with cloudy skies and bursts of rain that turned the sector into the sea of mud so often remarked in descriptions of the Meuse-Argonne. For some reason this weather did not afflict the men in the pocket. Not that they were completely spared suffering from the elements. There was cold and occasional rain, but not the torrents that came down elsewhere. They had no raincoats, although perhaps the lack was no deprivation, for AEF raincoats were notorious for their inability to shed water. They had no pup-tent shelter halves, which buttoned at the top, could be shared by two men, and might have been used for protection not merely against rain but also against the cold of the ground in the funkholes.

At 10:35 a.m. on October 4 Whittlesey released his fifth pigeon. Its message was received at the division message center at 11:30.

> Germans are still around us, though in small numbers. We have
> been heavily shelled by mortar this morning. Present effectives A,

B, C, E, G, H Cos.—175; K Co. 307th—45; Machine Gun detachment—17; total here about 235.

Officers wounded: Lt. Harrington, Co. A; Capt. Stromee, Co. C;
Lts. Peabody and Revnes, M.G. Battalion; Lt. Wilhelm, E Co., missing.

Cover bad if we advance up the hill and very difficult to move
the wounded if we change position. Situation is cutting into our
strength rapidly. Men are suffering from hunger and exposure; the
wounded are in very bad condition. Cannot support be sent at
once?

Whittlesey
Major, 308th Inf.

The mortar situation worsened with the arrival of two light mortars (*Minenwerfers*). The Germans put them in position, one slightly
to the right front, the other to the left. Holderman described the
mortar fire as nibbling torture.

Whittlesey's message spoke of some consideration of change of
position. It seemed inadvisable, for to the west the German position
was protected by machine guns; it was from the left flank that guns
bore in on the brook below and on the men in burial parties and
generally everyone in the pocket. Those guns served also to protect
the large mortar, itself covered by a dedicated machine gun. To the
north and east there was danger of encountering a barrage from
American artillery, for Whittlesey had reported his coordinates. The
hills to the south were objectionable because of their exposure to
German artillery fire, which came down there each day. The pocket
at least was protected from hostile artillery fire and fairly protected
from the large trench mortar to the northwest. And just how was
Whittlesey to get his wounded out of the pocket in case of a move,
in any direction? Thinking about a change probably had the value of
occupying time, a sort of intellectual exercise during increasingly
dull hours, supporting the original choice of the pocket late in the
afternoon of October 2.

By far the most disturbing, and harmful, event of Friday, October
4, was firing upon the pocket by American artillery, which started
at 2:45 and lasted an hour and thirty-five minutes. The friendly fire
opened auspiciously, beginning at the top of Hill 198 and ranging
down to Charlevaux Brook, all to the good, and bad luck for German
snipers in the area. Reaching the brook, it brought up geysers of
water and mud and produced widening puddles, as if the ground were

being showered by rocks. The fire was a combination, the men noticed, of high explosives, which dug holes, and shrapnel, the latter dropping shards of jagged steel.

But then the fire became unfriendly, indeed very much so. It walked right up into the pocket and stayed there. Nothing sufficed but to hunker down and wait it out, flattening if at all possible. If the men thought of getting out of the funkholes, they thought once more, for enemy machine gun and rifle fire was waiting. The big mortar opened up.

The result was appalling. The artillery fire uprooted underbrush and cut branches off trees, making the entire position more open to observation and sniper fire. Thirty men were killed or wounded. Whittlesey reported in his after-action paper that a few men either in confusion or purposely left the position and were all killed or else wounded and captured. These were casualties the force could ill afford.

The cause of the disastrous friendly fire was never investigated. It must have been a miscalculation of Whittlesey's coordinates by General McCloskey's regiments. As the pigeon messages came back they were typed out and sent around, but those copies seem to have been correct. One can suspect that if the records of any of McCloskey's regiments contained errors for the coordinates they surely would have turned up and something would have been said about it. Or, of course, the offending paper or papers might have disappeared on purpose. One of the light regiments, the 306th Field Artillery, fired its guns on October 4, and the coordinates were set out in the regiment's records as 95.56–77.00, 95.6–76.9, and 95.0–75.8, none of which were Whittlesey's coordinates. The colonel of the 306th might have asked the other regiments to engage in a show-and-tell of their records, but that did not happen. Or Whittlesey, upon surviving the five days in the pocket, might have insisted on at least a divisional investigation. But that did not happen either.

The lack of an investigation into the firing on the Lost Battalion seems all the more mysterious in light of another incident. When McCloskey's brigade fired on La Palette Pavillon on October 6–7, the 306th Field Artillery Regiment, which had fired on the above-mentioned coordinates on October 4, was accused of "wild firing," which led to a brigade, divisional, and corps investigation. A shell killed Second Lieutenant Harold Fiske of Company C, 306th Machine Gun Battalion, eight hundred meters, or a half mile, south of the 306th

Regiment's firing. An exhaustive investigation showed almost certainly that a German shell—the Germans were firing at the same time as the American regiment—killed young Fiske.[3] But the attention called to the death of Lieutenant Fiske surely would have brought an investigation of the 306th Field Artillery Regiment if the latter had been guilty of the wild firing on October 4 and, again, there was little thought of its having so fired. In the firing on the Lost Battalion, nothing ever was found.

There was the possibility, not a good one, that the shelling of the Lost Battalion was by French artillery. Because of the failure of the French Fourth Army to protect the Seventy-seventh's left flank, and the abject retreat from La Palette on October 2 in which it appears that an entire company was captured—after the war a German officer said his men took two hundred Frenchmen—there was criticism of the French for letting the Americans do the fighting. Holderman asserted that the barrage came from the southwest, over Binarville. He also claimed that the French commander on the left informed Alexander that a French plane reported no sign of the Lost Battalion, that the Americans had been killed or captured, and that enemy troops were concentrating in the area, so he was going to lay down an artillery concentration—and then, in spite of Alexander's objection, the French opened fire.

Where this story came from, how it could appear in a Fort Benning paper that Alexander presumably read before writing a letter of approval, is impossible to say. Holderman grouped the sources for his paper in an initial bibliography, but apart from his own experiences they were standard printed sources; apparently, he had no access to official or personal records. He prefaced his account of the barrage by relating that at 3:00 p.m. (Whittlesey said the barrage began at 2:45) a French plane came over the position and, despite enemy machine-gunning, continued to circle and then flew back toward the French lines—after which came the barrage.

In the midst of the shelling Whittlesey sent off his last pigeon message, his sixth. It was to be quoted by everyone who wrote about the Lost Battalion:

> We are along the road parallel 276.4. Our artillery is dropping a barrage directly on us. For heaven's sake, stop it.
>
> Whittlesey
> Major, 308th

The account by Johnson and Pratt made much of the fact that this message was by the last bird in Whittlesey's pigeon crate, which had been carted up to the pocket by Private Omer Richards.[4] Someone, perhaps Richards, had a story that heightened the drama, whereby when Whittlesey was ready for a pigeon Richards reached into the crate, and because he was so nervous a bird fluttered out. That left one pigeon, which someone named Cher Ami, and its exploit in taking the last message was celebrated within and without the AEF. Shot through the breast by enemy fire, a message capsule dangling from the ligaments of a shattered leg, it arrived in its loft, loyal to the Lost Battalion. It died of wounds in 1919 and then, suitably stuffed, went on exhibit in the Smithsonian Institution in Washington, D.C. The last pigeon bore the name of Cher Ami, but the story otherwise may be apocryphal. It is possible, however, that Richards did lose a pigeon. Apparently there were seven pigeons in the crate, and only six got back.

The arrival of Cher Ami seems to have had little to do with stopping the artillery fire. Whittlesey released the bird at the outset of the firing. The shelling of the pocket appears to have gone on until its ordained end, when the gunners decided to stop.

As had happened the day before, Friday saw two enemy attacks. The first came after the artillery barrage and again was from the crest of the hill above the pocket. The Germans came down with potato-masher grenades. The latter, fortunately, contained fairly small charges and if kept at a modest distance were tolerable. Attackers from the crest had to pass through the open area and cross the road, and the defending riflemen had excellent opportunity to take them out or turn them back, which once more they did.

The attackers employed a novelty in the second attack: it was after dark, 9:00 p.m. Flares shot up, across and around the position, turning night to day. From the sides and the front came the grenades. There were explosions all over the pocket. Nonetheless, after what the men had been through, the enemy attacks of October 4 caused little concern. The men assembled at firing lines and sent the attackers back.

Meanwhile, after 8:30 p.m., Chauchat fire could be heard from the south, clearly American fire.

2

The third day in the pocket, Saturday, October 5, began in the usual way. Patrols were put out, with no result save more dead and wounded. One patrol thought it saw two hundred Germans moving south to the hills in the rear.

By that time lack of food was the single deprivation that most affected the men. They could put up with much, but their energy was flagging, evident in the decision of the day before, which was no decision but recognition that no longer could they bury the dead. It is true that following a time of desire for what was not possible there could arise a sort of nirvana where somehow it seemed of less interest, less concern. This feeling had set in by the night of October 3, after the first day in the pocket, but the lack of interest did not prevent the effect of a lack of food, the increasing tiredness. Some men endured it more than others, or were better at putting up fronts.

It was on one of the days of the weekend, Saturday or Sunday, that Second Lieutenant Maurice S. Revnes buckled. Two dates are in the court-martial record, October 5 and 6. There was a court-martial on December 27, and the specification—required for any charge in a military court-martial—read that his offense occurred "in the Argonne Forest, on or about 5 October, 1918"; in another part of the record the date was October 6. The issue was over what the court considered lack of judgment, which one wonders might have been a symptom of the tiredness of all the command. For Revnes, defense of the pocket appeared to be a group sacrifice, with no hope of relief. It seemed pointless. He had been wounded, and continuing to hold out appeared inhuman because of the lack of a physician and medicine. In many cases gangrene had set in. The wounded were no longer able to contain themselves, to quietly endure their pain, and their cries could be heard by the Germans, who were encouraged by them. According to the court record Revnes thereupon "misbehaved." His offense was to send to Whittlesey the following note:

> If our people do not get here by noon, it is useless for us to keep up against these great odds. It's a horrible thing to think of, but I can see nothing else for us to do but give up—the men are starving—the wounded, like myself, have not only had no nourishment but a great loss of blood. If the same thought may be in your mind

perhaps the enemy may permit the wounded to return to their own lines. I only say this because I for one cannot hold out longer, when cornered as we are it strikes me that it is not a dishonorable deed to give up.[5]

That the lieutenant had sent the note there was no doubt. To the accusation that he had violated the Seventy-fifth Article of War, misbehavior on the field, and deserved dismissal from army service, he pleaded not guilty.

There is not much point in going into the details of the trial, which with its documentary annexes required twenty-nine double-spaced typescript pages. Almost all of it was testimony for the prosecution—the defense took little space, as the lieutenant's defender, an anonymous officer, put up no argument, no testimony, only objecting once to what he considered a hostile statement. The value of the court-martial record is the testimony of Captain McMurtry. It is highly descriptive, precise, and of course close to the event—the Lost Battalion had been out of the pocket only a few weeks. McMurtry made a surprisingly detailed statement. Having been a broker, he might have been expected to overstate what he and his fellow officers considered an effort to subvert the morale that he and Whittlesey and the others were trying to keep up. His testimony was levelheaded and in its detail fascinating, for he seemed to remember everything.

The only other prosecution witness was Holderman, and his statement was short, less than three pages. Whittlesey did not testify because he was in a hospital in Metz. The prosecution rested with the two testimonies and offered six pages of documents, none of them revealing. One was Whittlesey's after-action report of October 9.[6]

The court found Revnes guilty. For this offense the prosecution asked for and the court ordered his dismissal from the service. But he was not dismissed, which might have placed a stain upon his time in the army and affected his future as a civilian—he was not a Regular. For that reason, possibly, or because of the pettiness of the case, it underwent a review at General Headquarters by an officer of rank, Brigadier General James J. Mayes, who on February 18, 1919, reversed the verdict. The war was over, and General Mayes could have considered dismissal from the service only something that all officers commissioned out of civilian life were about to undergo as soon as ships were available to take them home. Mayes pointed out that Revnes was the surviving machine-gun officer (he was attached to the 306th Machine Gun Battalion) and knew the conditions that were affecting his own guns, which were increasing scarcity of ammunition and ever fewer men with machine-gun training to fire them. This militated in favor of considering surrender. "And for the further reason that as established by uncontradicted medical testimony the accused from the nature of his wound suffered continuous pain progressive in intensity from October 3, and . . . was necessarily thereby lowered in mentality and morale. In the foregoing case of Second Lieutenant Maurice S. Revnes the evidence shows that the accused gallantly performed his duty for many days under the most trying circumstances; that he was wounded and had for a long time been without food."[7]

To return to Saturday, October 5. Early that morning two planes came over bearing a message that the men in the pocket never received: "Hold out in your present position. Help is being sent you." Colonel Hannay the evening before had telephoned the Air Service representative at First Corps that he was sending down a message he wanted dropped by plane to the companies of the 308th Infantry. The message came in at 2:00 a.m., October 5, and went immediately to the Fiftieth Aero Squadron. At daylight the planes went up, one with three copies, and dropped them at 294.6–276.3, or so they believed. The copies all fell into German hands.

If this word had been received it would have served to boost morale, after the experience with the barrage. Headquarters, Seventy-seventh Division, must have known of the barrage by then. It was a good message to send.[8]

Another message from Hannay went out that night, in not altogether identical texts sent to the Air Service at 5:00, 5:15, and 5:30 p.m.: "Retire with your forces to regimental P.C. The attention of the enemy in your rear is being held by our rifle and machine-gun fire. This should enable you to locate the enemy by his fire and strike him in the rear and flank."[9] Like the first message of that day, this one fell in enemy lines. It was just as well. Whittlesey and McMurtry could not move their force, considering the apparently overwhelming size of the enemy force, the lack of protection from enemy artillery, and the danger of being fired on by American artillery. To abandon the wounded and now the unburied dead ran counter to all the traditions of the U.S. Army, and other armies for that matter, including the German foes who every night removed their dead and wounded, so far as they could, from around the pocket.

The wounded made every thought of a breakout impossible. And there was a second problem with the wounded, which Whittlesey and McMurtry did not consider. It became clear later, after the nearby Thirty-fifth Division was relieved by the First Division. The latter advanced over ground relinquished by the Thirty-fifth and discovered many dead who had been wounded in the retreat and were able to care momentarily for their wounds, using bandages from first-aid kits. Instead of the Germans picking them up with stretcher parties and taking them back to their own rear area, to field hospitals, they left them to die, which the men did.

The account of the Lost Battalion in the book by Johnson and Pratt, which contains many errors, but collected stories that may have been true, has a story about a copy of the message of Saturday evening that, true or not (there is no record in the National Archives or in the collections of personal papers at the War College in Carlisle Barracks), is worth telling. The copy, they wrote, turned up in the Seventy-seventh's papers with an annotation of the man who picked it up, "Dropped at Supply Co. 307 Rond Champ." A marginal comment was in the hand of General Alexander: "Seems to have been dropped too far south!!!" Rond Champ was seven miles behind the lines.[10]

Even though the defenders never received the messages, a development had occurred at 10:00 a.m. that made their hearts leap. It started as another misdirected barrage, opening at the crest of Hill 198, coming down the south side of Charlevaux valley, striking the marsh and brook, and producing more geysers. The men prepared for the worst. But the barrage lifted. It jumped, rose to the Binarville-Apremont road, and moved into the German positions at the crest. It appeared to be an extraordinary performance by American gunners. To the defenders, looking for proof the division was coming, it said that their position had been known all along, despite Friday afternoon, that one or all of the pigeon messages had gotten through.

Yet, like the unfriendly barrage of the day before, there was a mystery about this succeeding and perfect barrage that never was solved and, if only for purposes of history, should have been. After the rescue of the Lost Battalion the Seventy-seventh Division became involved in an attack on Grandpré and in the war's last days entered into the attack toward Sedan. Generals Alexander and McCloskey and all the other senior officers might well have been too busy to look into the artillery fires of October 4 and 5, into what had made the difference between them, why after the disastrous firing of October 4 the artillery brigade could manage so successful a fire on the morning of October 5—and not produce another accident. And if it could be so successful, why did it not do far more to protect the men in the pocket from the surrounding Germans? If the brigade could produce a perfect fire, on purpose, it could have surrounded Whittlesey's men with an artillery cordon, south, north, east and west, pounding the Germans unmercifully. McCloskey could have thrown up fire three or four times a day, at unpredictable intervals, catching all attempts by the attackers to come back into their positions. No one, as was mentioned in regard to the fire on October 4, looked into why history went the way it did.

At 4:00 p.m. German machine guns opened, perhaps in retaliation for what had happened that morning. They could have been fatal to Whittlesey and McMurtry, who were saved by chance as described by McMurtry in the Revnes trial:

> Major Whittlesey and I were seated in our funkhole which was situated a little above and toward the left flank of the funkhole where Lieut. [Marshall G.] Peabody was lying. This was on the late afternoon of the 5th of October. This was the second funkhole that we had taken. Our first one we occupied the night of the 2nd, 3rd, and 4th, and the artillery barrage had cut so much cover from below that we decided to move up on the slope. We thought this place that we had picked out would be a pretty good one and we were waiting for momentary attacks all the time. Some ranging shots were put over by the machine guns on the left flank and Lieut. Peabody said to us, "I think you have picked out a rather exposed position, you'd better look out." Well, we decided that probably he was right and that we would move from there to the left on the slope where there was a little slight hummock of ground, I should say about six inches high. The ranging shots became very steady and more continuous this time and Major Whittlesey and I lay down behind this hummock of ground with our heads toward our left flank. We had no more than taken our position on the ground than over came the machine-gun barrage, which was most

severe. It continued, I should say for probably sixteen or eighteen minutes, but it was most intense. You could hear the crackle of the machine guns and you could almost feel it in your face and they covered the slope with this heavy fire for a period, as I said, of about sixteen or eighteen minutes.[11]

What might have happened had the two battalion commanders been killed in their former funkhole one hesitates to think. It is possible that without the steadiness of the major and the captain, Revnes's suggestion to surrender might have been acted upon.

The Germans made another attack that day from the crest with their accustomed weapons, potato mashers. Beyond these bare details, the record says nothing. Of course, the attack failed.

During the day the sound of firing from the rear, the main force to the south, was clear. That night it became faint. McMurtry suggested to Whittlesey, who followed with an order, that company commanders occasionally, in a calm, let off eight or nine shots from a Chauchat, in hope the sound might carry to the division. This would say that the Lost Battalion was still there.

four The Gathering Solutions

Relieving the Lost Battalion was no simple task and occurred in stages that are difficult to keep in mind. The men of Whittlesey's force looked forward to relief by the main force of their division, and as they heard the sounds of the Springfields and Chauchats they kept up their hopes. On October 2, Wednesday, when the battalions of the 308th Infantry went into the pocket, General Alexander had no idea they would need relief, only reinforcement, and their brigade commander, General Johnson, seeing Whittlesey make the only advance in the entire First Army, to where he and Alexander had told him to go, could rightly feel that Alexander was off his back. On Thursday, October 3, below the Lost Battalion, Colonel Stacey of the 308th and Lieutenant Colonel Houghton of the 307th tried twice, unsuccessfully, to get through. The next day, Friday, October 4, Stacey protested that he did not have enough troops to break through and asked Johnson to be relieved of his command. The brigade commander directed Stacey to attack and refused his personal request but told Alexander about it. On Saturday morning, October 5, at 11:30, the division commander relieved Stacey and ordered Johnson to lead the attack, which Johnson did that afternoon, and also the following morning, Sunday, October 6, with no better results than Stacey.

General Johnson on Friday, October 4, had directed Houghton of the 307th to send a battalion to the east, where it could go around the German flank and then work its way forward into the Charlevaux valley and from there move west to Whittlesey. This effort, often attributed to Houghton, at first went slowly and only began to move on the following Monday, October 7. The prospect of its success was so slim that after his second futile attack on Sunday morning Johnson drafted a message to General Alexander entitled "Further Use of 154th Inf. Brigade in Action," asking relief of the brigade. He may not have sent it; a copy is in the division files, dated October 7, the day the Lost Battalion was relieved.[1]

In the accounts of relief, credit always goes to Houghton's flank battalion. This, however, is mistaking appearance for reality, for credit should go to the First Corps divisions to the right of Alexander's Seventy-seventh, the First and Twenty-eighth Divisions, together with part of a brigade of First Corps's reserve division, the Eighty-second. The First Division led off in First Army's general attack of October 4, succeeding that of September 26, by racing its left regiment north and somewhat west to just below the town of Fléville, considerably above the Lost Battalion. In relieving the Lost Battalion this move was the most important. The Twenty-eighth followed by taking the German strong point, Le Chêne Tondu. A brigade of the reserve Eighty-second thereupon moved up the Aire, and part of it made a ninety-degree turn into the heights of the Argonne, threatening to outflank the Germans in the forest. During this operation the men could hear the rumble of trucks and wagons carrying the defenders' artillery and supplies and whatever else they could get out, in haste, for the Americans were coming.

1

In his attack of Thursday and Friday, October 3–4, Colonel Stacey could bring up only a few men, for the bulk of the 308th was in the pocket. General Johnson gave him the brigade reserve, the Third Battalion of the 308th, and with Companies D and F of the First and Second battalions he mustered perhaps two hundred and fifty men. With too small a force, he necessarily failed. Johnson then tried twice, on Saturday afternoon, October 5, and Sunday morning, October 6, using the division reserve, the Third Battalion of the 307th, less Company K. How many men were in that battalion is uncertain. Captain Rich of the First Army inspector's office believed companies numbered no more than seventy men, which accorded with company strength in the pocket. The division reserve battalion had not had much rest after the Seventy-seventh's attack into the

Argonne on September 26. So adding it to the two hundred and fifty men Stacey had left in the 308th did not result in a large force, the sort of heavy force that might have created a volume of fire in front of the German line across the ravine to permit a close enough examination to discover a gap, if there was one.

In his memoirs Alexander was quite unfair to Stacey about the colonel's relief. The memoirs were an interesting production, published the same year, 1931, as Pershing brought out his own account, *My Experiences in the World War.* Alexander's memoirs were careful about Pershing, as former AEF commanders needed to be, for Pershing still could exert influence in the army, had a long memory, and did not like argument that reflected on his actions in 1917–1918. Alexander quoted a commendatory Pershing letter about the Seventy-seventh's management during the war. Such letters were of course boilerplate, and there must have been an underling in Pershing's General Headquarters office who wrote them by the dozen. In his memoirs the division commander took care to agree with everything Pershing did. The memoirs were assertive, however, about the failures of lesser commanders within the division.

In between descriptions of terrain and battlefield scenes, the memoirs made their individual criticisms. The trouble with Stacey, his division commander said, was that he moved too slowly. At the outset, on the morning of Thursday, October 3, it was absolutely necessary for him to get his men into the gap between the trenches on either side of the ravine, up which Whittlesey had gone, before the Germans closed the gap with wire. "Conjectures as to what might have happened," Alexander began, "are rarely profitable." Having said that, he resorted to an unfair conjecture. Stacey should have moved early in the morning before the wiring. "Had that been done (and there is every reason to believe that the path was open until about 9 a.m. on the morning of the 3rd) the mission of the division would probably have been completely fulfilled."[2]

The trouble with this conjecture, of course, was that early on the morning of October 3 no one in command quite understood what was going on. But a dozen and more years after the armistice, Alexander felt safe in his contention. The division commander had asked too much of Stacey, as anyone would have seen from the situation of the 308th on October 2–7, 1918. And the colonel had gotten himself into a corner for another reason. He may well have suffered a mental breakdown—whatever happened, the appearance was there.[3]

Stacey had gone to the Seventy-seventh after an unfortunate experience with the Third Division, where he had been a regimental commander. According to that division's commanding general, Major General Beaumont B. Buck, Stacey had turned his regiment into a quarreling, distrustful unit. He arrived early in August and asked for relief of ten officers for inefficiency; he said the regiment needed discipline, which may have been true, considering its poor record under Buck when it went into the Meuse-Argonne. In any event, Buck sent to the regiment a lieutenant colonel known to be reliable, he said, and Stacey claimed the new officer was obstinate, pigheaded, and pessimistic, the last being a prime fault for any officer of the AEF, according to Pershing. At that juncture Buck wanted Stacey out, and using his authority as division commander got him out, whereupon First Army posted Stacey to the Seventy-seventh.

Arriving at Alexander's division, the colonel appeared highly nervous, and on the day after his first attack he lost control of himself. He did not wish to send troops forward again, he said, and his reasons in that regard were certainly valid, for the attacks were futile. He made the mistake of telling Johnson so. The latter had little recourse but to insist that Stacey send the troops, for he was under pressure from Alexander. Stacey meanwhile told someone, apparently Johnson, that he wished he was in the Services of Supply, away from the front line. Johnson told Alexander that Stacey had said that, and added that he, Johnson, did not want to relieve him. Alexander demanded his relief, and Stacey went to the rear.

Stacey's future in the army—he was a Regular, with two citations for bravery—was finished. He was examined in the divisional rear area and sent back to a hospital. Alexander brought a case against him. Stacey was not present to defend himself, and the First Army backed the division commander. Stacey on October 21 went home on the transport *Kroonland*. Four days later, while at sea, he was demoted to his Regular rank of lieutenant colonel.

Battlefield fatigue, nervous breakdown, a psychiatric case—no one could be sure what had happened. Stacey's trouble with Buck, whatever it was, constituted no proof of anything, as Buck himself was relieved for incompetence (under the pretense that General Pershing was sending him home to train troops). Stacey simply may have been too frank in speaking with Johnson. In later years he did his best to clear his record, but it was impossible. In 1920, Major

John C. H. Lee, who had been a colonel and chief of staff of the Eighty-ninth Division in the Meuse-Argonne and would become a lieutenant general in World War II as General Dwight D. Eisenhower's supply chief during the invasion of France, took on Stacey's case, as he believed him the goat of the Lost Battalion's entrapment in the Argonne. He wrote the aide of General Pershing, Major (formerly Colonel) John G. Quekemeyer, asking Pershing's intervention. The former commander in chief was now army chief of staff. Whether Quekemeyer asked Pershing is impossible to say, but he responded to Lee that there was nothing to do for Class B officers, in which category Stacey had been placed.[4]

Stacey may have been Alexander's goat, as Lee suspected. He may have been incompetent, unable to control men in battle situations where there has to be control, with the men unable to escape the battlefield, everyone in place and subject to call. This meant using battle police on all rear areas to prevent straggling; the tendency of men to stray from the front was the curse of First Army in the Meuse-Argonne. Liggett estimated that there were one hundred thousand stragglers after the first attack. He was philosophical about it, writing that straggling was part of army life, that after the Civil War, on the western frontier, where he spent his early years in the army, he constantly had to go back and round up stragglers, with the errant men always full of ingenious excuses and, when no one was looking, returning to their ways. Under Stacey, straggling from the front was serious. Colonel Joseph I. Baer of the inspector general's office saw it and commented in his diary for October 4 that he had a report from a lieutenant colonel, Gordon V. Johnson from First Corps, that men in the front line were going back to the rear through the woods; the lieutenant colonel had gone up to the front and walked along the line and seen the problem. According to this informant, men on the line were themselves making no effort to do anything, just lying around, which amounted to straggling and assuredly bore the same result.[5]

Sensing the lack of command under the colonel, relieving him because of the comment about the Services of Supply, Alexander meanwhile had turned on his brigade commander. On October 2, before Whittlesey's companies began their move forward to the pocket, the division commander called Johnson on the field telephone and pushed him to obtain the same result that Whittlesey soon achieved. Johnson was out. "You tell General Johnson," Alexander told Johnson's artillery liaison officer, Captain M. G. B. Whelpley, "that the 154th Brigade is holding back the French on the left and that it is holding back everything on the right, and that the 154th Brigade must push forward to their objective today. By that I mean must, and by today I mean today—not next week. You report heavy machine-gun fire and determined resistance [he said to the staff officer, to galvanize him and Johnson's other staff officers] but the casualty lists do not substantiate this. Remember that when you are making these reports."[6]

Later that day Johnson himself received orders by telephone to the same effect. Alexander told him that if he, Johnson, could not handle the matter, then he, the division commander, would find someone who could.

The result was that after Stacey's relief Johnson himself went up to the front and led two attacks, on Saturday afternoon, October 5, and again the next morning. Alexander wanted him to attack a third time, but Johnson said it could not be done—he needed fresh troops, his left flank was open, and he needed to get in touch with the French, who were supposed to be in support. All the troops he had were Stacey's two hundred and fifty, less casualties, and the division reserve, the Third Battalion of the 307th, initially used on October 2.

While Johnson was attacking with these troops on the left, Houghton was attempting with his two remaining battalions to attack on the brigade right, with no more success.

The attacks of Stacey and Johnson to relieve the Lost Battalion were very costly, considering the numbers of men involved as well as the numbers in the pocket. Johnson told the First Army inspector, Captain Rich, that the chaplain told him that he took out a hundred bodies and had not gotten all of them. During the whole of the siege of the pocket it was estimated that the Lost Battalion had sixty-nine dead or missing.

Two and one-half years later, when General Johnson was Colonel Johnson and military attaché in Rome, he wrote General Pershing about a personal matter, two medals he desired, and in a long letter set out what he did when he led the attacks.[7] According to Johnson, when Alexander called on October 2 and, finding Johnson gone, left the message and hectored Captain Whelpley, Johnson had gone over to see Houghton. It was there that Johnson perfected his scheme by which the 307th's right battalion would flank the German line, find a break similar to the break between the trench lines that Whittlesey's men had found, and get into the Charlevaux valley and turn east into Whittlesey's position. This course, which the colonel followed on the sixth and seventh, seemed the key to reaching the besieged companies.

In his letter Johnson said he returned to his headquarters and upon Stacey's relief went himself to the brigade front. Arriving at the line below the Lost Battalion, Johnson tightened everything, so if a breakthrough there became possible he would command it. He told the 308th's new commander, Captain Lucian S. Breckinridge, that there was to be another attack and to assemble the officers of the companies available and of the division reserve, and he would give them detailed instructions. When the group came together he said he had come up himself to plan the attack and felt the chance of success was good if officers and men carried out his instructions. The line was four hundred yards in front of their location at regimental headquarters. When he announced another attack, following the losses under Stacey, he saw by the expression on the faces of the officers that they thought it hopeless, that unless he led them personally the attack would be perfunctory, so he said, "Gentlemen, I am going forward with you, and I am going to lead this attack in person. Our chances are good and we can break that line and get our comrades out of the hole they're in." He turned to Breckinridge: "Captain, you come with me and give orders to your senior officer to bring the troops forward."

Johnson and Breckinridge went up close, as far as they had cover, and Breckinridge brought the men forward. The time was 2:00 p.m. Troops gradually worked up to the line, Johnson himself to within twenty-five or thirty yards to see if he could find a weak place in the wire. He was under shelling and machine-gun and rifle fire; bullets cut his clothes. The fighting lasted until dusk, with no break found in the wire. Johnson drew the men back, under instruction, he said, from the division commander.

The next morning, Sunday, October 6, after a brief artillery preparation, Johnson again took the troops forward, personally exposing himself on the line to encourage officers and men. His left flank was open except for a few troops to guard against infiltration. The French were nowhere to be seen. The attack failed.

Alexander wanted an attack on Monday, October 7. The previous afternoon Johnson learned that Houghton was slipping men of the 307th's right battalion through a gap in the German line, and on Monday evening the 307th relieved the Lost Battalion.

Johnson may have done as well as anyone could. His reports are wonderfully clear and detailed. Like Alexander, he had his detractors among his fellow general officers. The other brigade commander in the Seventy-seventh, Wittenmyer, told Liggett's aide, Pierpont L. Stackpole, that Johnson was a liar. Major General George B. Duncan of the Eighty-second wrote in his memoirs that when he was in command of the Seventy-seventh, before Alexander, he had gone off for a day and upon return discovered that Johnson had allowed a company commander to take his men across no-man's-land into the German line in broad daylight, with the purpose of capturing prisoners, with the result that instead nearly the entire company was captured. Duncan complained to corps and showed his complaint to Johnson before sending it in. Inspectors appeared, and their report disappeared. Nothing happened. But however one interprets these commentaries, Johnson appears to have done his best on October 5–6. He simply did not have enough troops to accomplish anything.[8]

One does wonder why Alexander, who in his memoirs insinuated that Johnson had not done everything he could, did not relieve him instead of hectoring him. After Alexander called Johnson on the telephone and ordered him to advance, and said that if Johnson could not do the job he would find someone who could, the brigade commander, Johnson, telephoned the division chief of staff, Colonel Hannay, and told him that if the division commander did not like his work he could relieve him at any time. Alexander could have put Houghton in as brigade commander; rank would not have been a concern in replacing a brigadier general with a lieutenant colonel, since the 308th then was commanded by a captain.[9]

Instead, Alexander seems to have sulked and done not as much as Johnson, who was at the front. There is no record of the major general going up to the front to see conditions. Alexander's headquarters appears to have possessed little understanding of what was going on there. Hannay sent the message to Whittlesey, never received, to fight his way back, this without appreciation for the difficulties Whittlesey and McMurtry faced in moving. Before that, on October 4, G-4 of division headquarters, the supply corps, sent up

food and ammunition for the Lost Battalion to Stacey's and Johnson's line, with no sense that, given the way the attacks were going,
there was no way to get it up to the pocket.

Alexander on October 5 took time out to visit First Corps headquarters and talk to Liggett, this when Johnson was attempting his
first personally led attack. Alexander told the corps commander,
and the interview was recorded by Liggett's aide Stackpole, that he
was about at the end of his rope.[10] He asserted that he had tried
coaxing and kicking and every expedient to make his men move.
Losses, he said, were not heavy, and he had the stragglers, many of
them. He thought the 154th Brigade was not all used up. He was
greatly distressed that he could report no better progress. He said
the tactical developments on his left, those of the 154th, were the
worst he ever saw. He had just canned another colonel (Stacey),
given the regiment to a captain, and companies were down to one
officer apiece.

Stackpole thought the Seventy-seventh's commander was having
an unusual amount of trouble with officers and was acting hastily
on their shortcomings. He heard Alexander say nothing good about
any of them except "old Wit," who himself eventually requested re-
assignment from the division and told Stackpole he hated Alexander. Put off by this, Stackpole wrote, "One gets the impression that
he stands quite alone in the whole show." A reader, years later, gets
the impression that in visiting Liggett, who incidentally told the
Seventy-seventh's commander he was doing everything he could,
Alexander was building a case for losing the Lost Battalion.

2

The first of the moves from outside the Seventy-seventh Division
that saved the Lost Battalion was not for the purpose of saving
Whittlesey's men but had a marked effect in helping Whittlesey.
This was the move forward of the First Division on October 4, the
day of Pershing's general attack by First Army. The First Division,
the "Big Red One," had come into line after the defeat of the Thirty-
fifth, which had been the right division in First Corps, to the right of
the Twenty-eighth, which in turn was the Seventy-seventh's right-
hand neighbor. The subsector of the Thirty-fifth ran from the Aire to
a line east of Vauquois Hill and Cheppy. The Thirty-fifth's five days

in the field, September 26 to the night of September 30–October 1, when the First took over, had started out well but turned extremely unhappy, for its brigade commanders lost control of their regiments, and by September 29 the regiments were in disorder approaching collapse. The division lost Exermont and Montrebeau Woods. It was saved by a defense line established from Baulny and running to the northeast, held by twelve hundred men of the 110th Engineer Regiment, together with such retreating infantrymen as engineer and other officers could gather. At the same time the heavy guns of First Corps and First Army put down a protective arc of fire.[11]

The primary purpose for the presence of the First Division was to roll back the Germans from the territory the Thirty-fifth had lost, but the division was expected to do a good deal more than that. The collapse of the Thirty-fifth had been caused not by machine-gun nests ahead of the troops but by artillery fire from high up in the whaleback, as it was called, the middle of the Meuse-Argonne sector, where there were hills all the way north to Buzancy, and from, more particularly, sixteen German batteries emplaced in the heights of the Argonne around Châtel-Chéhéry. When Pershing opened his second attack, the First Division was to surge forward and if at all possible get up to Fléville, along the Aire, farther than the Thirty-fifth, which had only made it for a brief moment to Exermont. From Fléville the First could threaten the German artillery positions near Châtel-Chéhéry. The batteries there had to be taken out, for they were enfilading First Army all along the line. The batteries on the whaleback were of less moment, and as the battle continued were shoved farther back where, if not out of range, they could do less harm, firing from the limits of their range.

The guns around Châtel-Chéhéry were well placed in the ground in that area of the Argonne, where the soil contained a great deal of limestone. The Germans had only to dig this ground for emplacements; the ground was so hard from the limestone that it was not necessary to revet the emplacements. Only direct or very near hits could take them out.

One might have thought that aviators could have obtained the guns' coordinates, allowing the American artillery to range in on them. Divisional artillery if out of range could call on the guns of corps and First Army. It was a good idea in theory, but in practice not easy. After the first day in the Meuse-Argonne the Air Service squadrons assigned to First Army lost control of the air to the skilled German pilots. Air Service pilots were not practiced in working with division commanders. In the cases of the green divisions there had been no opportunity. Some artillerymen, such as Brigadier General Lucien G. Berry of the Thirty-fifth, were heard to say that planes were "no damned good," and they had to be tutored in working with them, as Berry was by September 29, too late for him and his division.

The First Division when it attacked did its best, which considering the obstacles was very good. It was stalled after the first day, like the others, and had to mop up, which included capturing the hill above Exermont, the Montrefagne. But its left regiment passed around the Montrefagne on up to Fléville, a splendid advance. It did not try to hold the town, which would have exposed it to artillery fire, and chose a ravine slope just below where the men were safe and could take the town whenever they desired.

The First Division's advance was magnificent, but the cost of the operation was high. The cost lay not in the advance to Fléville but in earlier and later casualties. When the division was waiting for the new offensive to begin it necessarily placed its troops in ravines, and the Germans filled the ravines with gas, creating hundreds of casualties. After the attack it was necessary to take the Montrefagne and to bring up the rest of the division line parallel to Fléville, in order to prevent the enemy from flanking the town, and those actions were costly. The casualties mounted until they may have reached seven thousand, higher than those suffered by the defeated Thirty-fifth Division that the First replaced. The First was under command of a Pershing favorite, Major General Charles P. Summerall, who critics said would push men straight into anything—all right for Summerall's reputation but not for his men's survival. Summerall, however, who if in conversation sometimes was the George S. Patton Jr. of World War I, was, like Patton, a thoughtful officer who knew when to push. The army's leading artillerist, he understood the power of the big guns and sought not to attack unless his men had artillery protection. If necessary, on occasion, and he considered October 4 one of them, he would push and take the casualties. He had tight control of his brigades and regiments, unlike Major General Peter E. Traub of the Thirty-fifth, who lost control during the first day, September 26. Fléville fell to irresistible force. The First

Division threatened the batteries near Châtel-Chéhéry. And it did something of less moment but distinctly worthwhile. Because the First was so near the Argonne, word came down from German headquarters to Wellmann, whose regiment had surrounded the Lost Battalion, that headquarters could not assume the safety of his troops beyond a day or two. Word arrived on October 5 to retire the next day. Wellmann asked for and received a reprieve of a day, through October 7, not enough for his regiment to take the *Amerikanernest.*

The way in which Summerall disheartened the enemy in the Argonne was not at all clear to those at the headquarters of First Army, and especially to General Liggett, who was beside himself that he seemed not to be getting the enemy batteries, at the same time as the enemy surrounded two battalions of the Seventy-seventh. It was at this point that he had an idea that, had it been possible to carry out in its entirety, might have changed everything in the Meuse-Argonne and brought victory far sooner than actually happened (which was with First Army's final attack of November 1–11). He talked the idea over with his chief of staff, Brigadier General Malin Craig, who called the chief of staff of First Army, later Brigadier General Hugh A. Drum, who cleared things with General Headquarters. The idea was to send the Eighty-second Division, in corps reserve, up the road along the Aire, Route Nationale No. 46, the only decent road in the entire Meuse-Argonne, to a place above Apremont, then turn the division, together with such troops as were available from the Twenty-eighth Division, into the Argonne heights, to get the guns and drive far enough into the forest to cut off the Germans in the Argonne, in the process relieving the Lost Battalion. The idea was so startling in its attractiveness that the historian of the AEF, Edward M. Coffman, has described it as the single tactical innovation of the entire battle of the Meuse-Argonne.

The plan was agreed to at a hasty luncheon conference at First Corps on October 6. Present, in addition to Liggett, were Drum; Pershing's chief of staff, McAndrew; perhaps the G-3 of General Headquarters, Brigadier General Fox Conner (afterward Drum was uncertain of this, Liggett certain); Duncan of the Eighty-second; and Duncan's chief of staff, Colonel Raymond Sheldon.

It is possible that the plan agreed to on October 6 was drawn up too quickly—the attack, in conjunction with regiments of the Twenty-eighth, was to take place the next morning, October 7. Duncan in his memoirs considered the meeting close to a farce, as he said that McAndrew seemed fixated on an eminence that the Twenty-eighth was to take, Hill 244, and could think of little else. He complained to his memoirs, not to the assemblage of generals including his corps commander, that no one had the slightest idea how the Eighty-second would get across the river, which if shallow was not all that passable, with depths of two to three feet. The Aire bridges long since had been blown. The meeting evidently was not a smooth affair, as Stackpole wrote that Duncan was slow-witted, "seems to be as thick as mud and not worth a damn and neither he nor Sheldon, his Chief of Staff, seem to have much conception of what they are expected to do in a tactical sense."[12] The result was something of a botch, in terms of what it might have been, and yet perhaps as good as the moment permitted. The period from the end of September through the middle of October was not a time when First Army showed a great deal of skill in attacks. It compared poorly to the German Army. Liggett was asking for more ability, as he afterward admitted, than his divisions possessed.

The problem, which Duncan had a few hours to solve, was to get the Eighty-second up and across the Aire. The division was at Varennes. Duncan chose to send a brigade rather than the division, as he had detached a regiment to assist the Thirty-fifth Division on its right flank. Even a brigade proved difficult. The men went up at night, and the passage up was unforgettable. Rain came down in torrents, and everyone was soaked. They wore their worthless AEF raincoats. The Germans across the river had the Route Nationale, the Neuvilly-Varennes-Apremont-Fléville-Grandpré road, under observation, with star shells from the heights turning night into an eerie sort of day. The road was full of trucks, wagons, and carts, and the men had to walk close to and into the ditches and try to avoid slipping into the slime.

The area into which the brigade was going was a no-man's-land wedged between the First Division and the Twenty-eighth. Patrols, American and German, penetrated it during the nights and confronted each other. As the men turned to the left, crossing the river into the forest, they were protected from enemy fire from the north because the ravines ran east-west, but not from batteries in the Argonne. Their right flank was exposed, in the air, and would have been in danger if the enemy forces had had enough troops to attack.

Because the Twenty-eighth Division did not provide the Eighty-second with scouts, it was said, although this was unclear, only two thousand men got across. Once across the river, into the Argonne, there were the heights. The Eighty-second's history relates, with pardonable pride, that "no more formidable natural fortifications are to be found on the entire battle front than the precipitous ridges extending from Châtel-Chéhéry and west of Cornay to the town of Marcq," the latter on the Aire as it turned west toward Grandpré.[13]

In the event the Eighty-second put across part of two regiments of the Sixty-fourth Brigade. The 327th Infantry had gone up the Varennes road in battle order, the lead battalion its First under an able man, Major F. W. Blalock. It arrived at a ford in the vicinity of La Forge at 3:00 a.m. and went across as best it could. Engineers placed boards from rock to rock, which worked for some men, and the others waded. Blalock stood on the west bank and helped them get up the slope. The battalion marched north and formed on the small-gauge railroad track east of Hill 180, the point of attack.

There is little reason to go into detail about the successive actions as the Eighty-second's brigade moved in on the Germans, reaching Hill 180, then Hill 223, and beyond to the Decauville small-gauge railroad (the Germans used such lines to supply troops in the Argonne). Duncan recalled the brigade's work with pride. Hill 223 fell on October 7 and the railroad the next day, after the Lost Battalion was relieved. That day the Tennessee mountaineer Corporal Alvin C. York performed what General Pershing described as one of the most astonishing individual feats of the war, capturing 128 Germans and killing two or three dozen with his rifle and pistol.

During the attack the weak regiments of the Twenty-eighth took Hill 244. With such actions on the heights of the Argonne, Wellmann did not have the means to stay any longer, and after a final attempt to overwhelm the Lost Battalion on the afternoon of October 7, his force surrounding Whittlesey got out as fast as it could. By dusk the Germans around the pocket were leaving as Houghton's men came in.

five   October 6–7

For the Lost Battalion the last two days in the pocket, Sunday and Monday, October 6–7, were the worst. Before that time there had been hope of relief—that the division would break through. But the disappointments accumulated. So did the weaknesses that came from lack of food; there was a progression downward, at first evident in intense hunger, then in a sort of nirvana, always with a lessening ability to withstand daily tasks, including the German attacks. The last days were about all the men could stand.

Being close together had advantages, for the men of weaker stamina could have support. At the same time, togetherness carried a price in bad temper and general impatience. Whittlesey's presence seems to have placed a kind of quietus on the men, for the major fascinated them; in their unspoken ways they adored him and would do everything they could for him. This had much to do with morale. McMurtry boosted morale in another way, with never a gloomy word, always encouragement, a quip or a bright remark that broke the continuing dullness and raised spirits.

1

Sunday, October 6, in the pocket, was no special day, with less going on than on the preceding days—although if the men could have known of the assembling of the conference of generals at Liggett's headquarters, and of his tactic of sending in the Eighty-second, up the Aire with a turn at La Forge, that would have raised spirits. They of course knew nothing, having had no contact with the outside since Cher Ami flew off, two days before.

The morning began with patrols. They were no more successful than preceding patrols at finding a weak place in the German line and breaking out. "It was just the same story," McMurtry said afterward. But the men made their best effort. A summary later for General Drum described the men as "exceedingly determined," for as the report to Drum had it their courage had been shaken by the failure of division troops to get through.[1]

The men were very hungry (they had a day and a half to go). Many asked permission to work their way back through at night. After the night of October 3–4 when a few shells fell into the position, the sleep of the men had been undisturbed, and the terrain surrounding the pocket made it tempting to believe that not much was out there, that a good man could get through while the Germans were sleeping. But the distance back was a kilometer, and failure to skirt the brush could create noise, or a misstep could loosen a rock. The capture of a man attempting to escape would undermine the appearance of defiance that Whittlesey wanted. Having sent word to the officers to tell the men this was a fight to the finish, he wanted the notion held to. The officers refused all requests.

That day Lieutenant Peabody of Company D, 306th Machine Gun Battalion, was killed. So was Lieutenant Alfred R. Noon of Company C. The number of officers was diminishing.

There was a single attack on October 6. No one remembered much about it, except that a potato masher struck Captain McMurtry; already wounded by shrapnel in the knee, he refused to be downed and carried on with the handle of the masher sticking out of his back.

A disturbing situation was developing in regard to machine-gun ammunition and machine gunners. Holderman on the right flank with what remained of Company K remembered that ammunition ran very low. The number of gunners was decreasing, and they were losing their officers, most recently with the death of Peabody. When General Mayes reversed the verdict of the court-martial of Lieutenant Revnes, it was in large part because the lieutenant had been wounded, which Mayes believed affected his judgment, but he took into consideration that Revnes as a machine-gun officer knew how short the ammunition and gunners had become and that without guns, especially on the left flank, the defenders would have been unable to put up enough fire to hold off the Germans.

The machine-gun situation may have been more dire than it appeared in retrospect to those trying to figure out what happened. Mayes had access to information that seems to have disappeared and in his reversal wrote that Sergeant George E. Hauck of the machine-gun battalion told Revnes of the state of affairs, that Sergeant Herman G. Anderson and a Private Foss said the same thing, and that on the morning of October 6 both guns on the left flank were out of commission while on the right only one of six was in service. Nine guns had gone into the pocket, and that report accounted, on this day, Sunday, for seven. The men also said ammunition sufficed for twelve minutes of continuous fire.

On the right, Holderman's men employed an expedient that brought in rifles and ammunition in lieu of the unusable machine guns. After dark they went out to the dead Germans around them. These were the dead the enemy could not carry back because they fell too close to the defending line. The men gathered rifles and ammunition from the bodies. They found the German rifles to be good sniping weapons, if not comparable to Springfields for long-range work.

The event on Sunday, indeed a series of events, was the attempted dropping of food, ammunition, medical supplies, and pigeons by the Air Service. None of the drops were successful. Everything fell into German positions. Nonetheless, it was pleasant to know that the Lost Battalion still was not lost, that the division knew where it was.

The Air Service outdid itself in trying to help. Considering that this was 1918, only fifteen years since the Wright brothers' feat at Kitty Hawk, what the service tried to do deserves praise. That the effort failed should not stand against it, since this was apparently the first effort at a sizable airdrop that the service attempted, perhaps the first that planes had tried.

Fourteen pilots and fifteen observers of the Fiftieth Aero Squadron took part. Planes dropped forty sacks by parachute, one thousand pounds, half a ton, and while the result was difficult to discern, the pilots felt good about it. The planes dropped two crates of pigeons and, to ensure soft landings, used as many as eight parachutes for each crate, taken from parachute flares.

There seemed something approaching a consensus that the pilots could see the Lost Battalion's identification panels, and it was likely that was so. The planes came in at a thousand feet, barely at the south and north crests. The Lost Battalion put out panels into late in the afternoon of October 7. Panels, incidentally, were standard procedure for units in the Meuse-Argonne, but use of them did not become common until a few weeks after the first attack of September 26. In the hapless Thirty-fifth Division, units went into action without panels. Only the two attack regiments had them; the other two regiments didn't. Some units could not find their panels. Officers had allowed men to tear them up as rags. Some signalmen improvised with underwear. And it was true that, even with panels, a unit could not be sure planes could find it. Seeing panels required low flying and attention to the ground, allowing enemy planes to come out of clouds, sail in unobserved, and take out planes. In the instance of Whittlesey's and McMurtry's battalions the two commanders were careful leaders who laid their panels out daily and made no such errors as leaving them behind.

To the pilots everything seemed to be working. An Air Service message of Sunday to Dreadnought 5, G-3—Alexander's operations officer, Lieutenant Colonel Howze—patted the Fiftieth Squadron on the back: "They feel pretty good about that, do they," asked the sender. He answered his own question: "Good work, that's fine business."[2]

Dreadnought 5 heard of drops at 1:20 p.m. Later, at 6:00, planes dropped six more messages carrying Colonel Hannay's earlier instruction, that the Lost Battalion try to fight its way back. None fell in the pocket.

As for why the drops all failed, there were several possibilities. One was the small size of the pocket. A report afterward spoke of dropping in the bottom of the valley, which would have missed the pocket, located up the north side. Another reason for missing might have been in measuring the effect of wind. Without practice, it was also likely that the effects of speed were not well accounted for— even in those days of slow air speed it was difficult to make allowance.

Despite pilots' belief that they saw panels, they may have calculated the drops by the fire put up by the Germans. The enemy force fired furiously. Such firing rarely worked but had the advantage of making gunners feel better. They did it if ammunition permitted, which that of the Germans did. Pilots may have seen this fire, part of which was from machine guns, and took it for signaling by the Lost Battalion. Or they may have seen the fire of the two light mortars, the *Minenwerfers.* Pilots thought they saw big white flares.

There may have been inability to determine coordinates from the air. American pilots had flown only a few weeks—the Air Service did not become operational until the late summer of 1918—and could have had trouble with coordinates. At 11:30 a.m. a returning plane reported 294.6–276.4, another at 2:45 gave 294.5–276.5. The real coordinates were 294.6–276.3. Differences were small but would have sufficed to put drops off center. It was one thing for artillery commanders, on the ground, to calculate coordinates, something else altogether to do it in the air.

In its effort of Sunday to help the Lost Battalion the Fiftieth lost two planes, both of which came down within American or French lines.[3] The one within French lines was shot down by German machine-gun and rifle fire. It resulted in the death of the pilot, First Lieutenant Harold Goettler, and the observer, Second Lieutenant Erwin Bleckley. Both received the Congressional Medal posthumously. Thus, the Lost Battalion inspired five Congressional Medals, the others going to Whittlesey, McMurtry, and Holderman. In addition to the two deaths in the aero squadron an observer, Lieutenant McCurty, was shot in the neck but survived to fly again. On October 6 squadron planes flew 184 hours.

Monday, October 7, was not merely misty, as had been the day of the big drop, Sunday, but raining, and the aero squadron sent up only four planes, with one finding the pocket and dropping another message, lost like all the others. The flight hours for Monday were only five.

After the drops of food, ammunition, medical supplies, and pigeons on Sunday, which all missed their mark, enemy troops shouted descriptions of what they had found, and the Americans replied with choice invectives.

At the end of Sunday, after the diversion of watching the aero squadron coming close to providing assistance, the men were feeling more tired and needed something to lift their spirits. They could not know that the First Division had broken the entire German position in the Aire valley. The German withdrawal would reach all the way west to the Aisne River. La Palette Pavillon had to be abandoned.

The sixteen batteries on the heights of the Argonne had to move back, even before the men of the Eighty-second were reaching for them with assistance from the Twenty-eighth. The next morning, October 7, when the Eighty-second attacked its first hill, the Germans were surprised because it anticipated their schedule. It gave an inconvenient push. Thereafter the two American divisions encountered rearguard actions as forces along the entire line pulled out.

General Wellmann knew that if he delayed getting his corps out he would take a chance of being surrounded. His men were at the apex of an inverted triangle—not a good position. But he was intent on capturing the Lost Battalion, almost as much as General Liggett was intent on getting it out, and asked for his extra day and received it. He asked for *Stosstruppen,* a battalion of attack troops for a special assault, and received only sixteen men when he needed at least one or two hundred. He decided to use them the next day, his last day.

2

The most interesting aspect of what happened on Monday, October 7, was not that it was the day of deliverance, which was so welcome, so emotional. Nor was it the events that preceded, which were of much interest, notably the second German attack of that day in which Wellmann and his regimental commander, Major Huenicken, put in the *Stosstruppen,* what few they had of them, who carried flamethrowers. It was that on this day, October 7, which ended with deliverance, the men of the Lost Battalion were at the virtual end of their resistance. Had there been another attack, it would have succeeded. The survivors of the Lost Battalion had the will, but they had almost nothing with which to defend themselves. By the end of the second attack ammunition was nearly gone. Of the nine Hotchkiss guns brought into Charlevaux valley, two were left. Holderman, who should have known, wrote that there were no gunners left to feed the remaining five boxes of ammunition. His statement is difficult to prove, for while there apparently were no machine-gun officers to continue at the guns, and the two sections of the 306th Machine Gun Battalion had 75 percent casualties, that would have left some men who could have handled the guns, presumably one on each flank or both on the left flank, which had been manned mostly by machine guns and where the Germans were stronger with their own machine guns. The ammunition for the Chauchats, rifles, and pistols was down, with not enough remaining to repel another attack. The grenades were all gone.

The men were seen sharpening bayonets by pushing them into the ground. In the Meuse-Argonne and in other actions of the AEF bayonets were of little use; because of enemy fire men so armed could not get close enough to engage their foes. Bayonets appeared ferocious, and in war posters and memorials, in stained-glass mosaics of attacking soldiers that adorned state capitols and other public places, or in sculptures, invariably men were shown plunging bayonets into protesting Germans. Surgeons in the AEF saw few bayonet wounds. The killers were artillery and, to a much lesser extent, machine guns and gas.

For the Lost Battalion, Monday, October 7, opened with shells falling on the position from the southeast. There were just a few, and they turned out to be the work of a single German gun that had gotten into a position where it could enfilade the pocket. The Germans were clever at placing artillery pieces and did not scruple to take what the Americans described as pirate guns into places from which they could not get them out, where after working them they abandoned them. The pirate gun fired for a while and stopped, the gunners getting out as fast as possible.

That day Lieutenant Gordon L. Schenck of C Company was killed.

At noon the Germans attacked and were driven off. No record of this attack, like that of the preceding day, seems to have survived. The men probably repelled it as if they were automatons, such work having become mechanical.

At 4:00 p.m. came something unexpected. This was a note sent across the lines asking the Americans to surrender. It was written by Lieutenant Fritz Prinz, who had spent four years in Spokane as a representative of a German company. He had returned to Germany in 1914 and, because he was a reservist, was called up. His division commander asked him to write a note proposing surrender.[4]

The carrier was a prisoner, Private Lowell R. Hollingshead, who with seven other men of Lieutenant William J. Cullen's Company H had crossed over behind the line, without permission, to see if they could find the food dropped by the Fiftieth Squadron. Four were killed, the others wounded and captured. Prinz selected Hollingshead, who received a stick and a piece of white cloth. Blindfolded, he was led out of the German position and released. The men in the pocket saw him coming and held fire.

The note he delivered read as follows:

> Sir:
>
> The bearer of this present, Lowell R. Hollingshead, has been taken prisoner by us. He refused to give the German Intelligence Officer any answer to his questions, and is quite an honorable fellow, doing honor to his Fatherland in the strictest sense of the word.
>
> He has been charged against his will, believing that he is doing wrong to his country to carry forward this present letter to the officer in charge of the battalion of the 77th Division, with the purpose to recommend this commander to surrender with his force, as it would be useless to resist any more in view of the present condition.
>
> The suffering of your wounded men can be heard over here in the German lines, and we are appealing to your humane sentiments to stop. A white flag shown by one of your men will tell us that you agree with these conditions. Please treat Lowell R. Hollingshead as an honorable man. He is quite a soldier. We envy you.
>
> The German Commanding Officer[5]

The response of Whittlesey was silence, although his apocryphal response was "Go to hell!" When Hollingshead arrived he was brought to the major, who was in the company of McMurtry and Holderman. Whittlesey read the note aloud. The three officers looked at each other and smiled, as they took the message as a sign the enemy was weakening, resorting to an appeal. Whittlesey told Hollingshead to go to his company, and that was that. When newspapermen at division headquarters asked General Alexander for Whittlesey's response he answered, "Why, I suppose, 'Go to hell!'" Such a response would have been out of character for Whittlesey, and in any event never occurred. But it made good newspaper copy.

After the note arrived, Whittlesey asked the men to take in the airplane panels, to prevent confusion as to their purpose. When the men in the pocket did not put up their white flags of surrender, another attack was not long in coming. Holderman, usually reliable, although he mixed the dates of the artillery barrages, unfriendly and friendly, and imagined a French barrage, wrote of guttural sounds around the position as the enemy prepared.

By all accounts this attack was the worst. The attackers, Holderman wrote, used their whole bag of tricks—*Minenwerfers,* potato mashers, snipers, and at the end flamethrowers. The grenadiers came over the crest. Enemy squads sought to infiltrate the left flank. The attack was reaching its height when liquid fire shot into the defending companies on the right flank, including Holderman's Company K. Saving the flamethrowers until the end, the attackers hoped they would bring all resistance to an end.

The flamethrowers employed in World War I were not complicated. They used a liquid, petroleum distillate, and coal-tar fraction that did not flame until it struck a target. *Stosstruppen* carried tanks and hoses that threw the liquid a hundred feet. Electricity or friction at the nozzle ignited it. "They say," Johnson and Pratt wrote with prescience in 1938, "that bigger and better *Flammenwerfers* have been devised for the next war."[6]

Men of the AEF believed the Germans introduced the practice of burning enemies to a crisp in the same spirit they introduced gas at Ypres in 1915 and fired the Paris gun indiscriminately for seventy miles in 1918. During the war the French Army adopted liquid fire, but the Americans refused to follow.

On the part of the defenders during this last attack something almost strange happened, a keying up of remaining energies for the occasion, a state of mind the Germans had not counted on. It began with questioning and answering, all around the pocket, inspired by the surrender note. The men called to each other, "What's that?" The answer was, "They want us to quit," with an explanation, "The major told them to go to hell." By a comprehensible reaction, Johnson and Pratt wrote, a mental chemistry, "every other emotion of the dead-weary, starving, wounded, hysterical men was transformed into a wild rage, a furious desire for vengeance."[7]

The result was a series of taunts shouted to the enemy employing all the epithets of New York City and those of states in the West including California. When it came, the attack seemed easier to repel than usual. According to Johnson and Pratt, and Holderman corroborated this, wounded men rose from funkholes and stumbled to the firing lines. Those who could not walk loaded rifles. Everywhere the attackers were forced back. According to the authors of 1938, on the right flank Holderman was the hero of the occasion, in the thick of the action, shooting with his pistol, "whooping with delight every time he hit a man."[8] Wounded again, he stayed on his feet and with the help of a sergeant broke the whole wave on his flank. On the left was something approaching a counterattack that sent a German platoon reeling, the officer killed, the men in disorder.

As for the flamethrowers, the later playwright Laurence Stallings, who lost a leg as a Marine officer at Belleau Wood and wrote an attractive history of the American Army in France, *The Doughboys: The Story of the AEF, 1917–1918*—had American machine gunners firing pointblank at the *Stosstruppen,* whom the liquid fire they were carrying turned into human torches.[9] Stallings brought to the book a writer's flair. He was none too careful with his narrative, filling it with errors. But American fire did stop the flamethrowers, riflemen picking off the men carrying the tanks of liquid. In this way the attack on the afternoon of October 7 came to an end.

Relief was on the way. The 307th had found a break in the wire. Delaware 1, General Johnson, sent the news to Dreadnought 1, General Alexander. He had just heard from Houghton, he said, whose advance elements "are now on the line 95.4–75.9 at 2 o'clock, and he is probably on 76 now."[10] The line Houghton needed was 76.3, the Charlevaux valley. Interestingly, the time was two hours before the surrender note, which was followed by the last German attack. The Lost Battalion was facing its largest trial alone.

Sending his message, Johnson added a comment about Germans ahead and to the left of Houghton: "I think they have probably had orders to get out all along, Sir. That's what it looks like." He added another comment, unusual in writing to his division commander: "You were doing the best you could. I understand."[11]

As Houghton's men advanced they came on Private Abraham Krotoshinsky. That morning, or it could have been the night before, Whittlesey had authorized Krotoshinsky and another private to attempt to get out, any way they could. Krotoshinsky stumbled into a deserted German trench. He lay quietly trying to regain strength and discover where he was. He heard American voices and, not having the password, began shouting, "Hello, hello."[12] A group of scouts found him. His arrival, to be sure, was late, and although he testified that he was taken to an officer, whom he informed of the location of the Lost Battalion, there was not much value in the message; the

307th's men were very close anyway and knew the coordinates of their quarry. For valor, and willingness to chance a passage that had defied all of their predecessors, Krotoshinsky and his fellow volunteer, who also survived but did not meet up with the 307th, received the Distinguished Service Cross.

From within the pocket, following the attack that afternoon, the men could see Germans hurrying to the rear. As Holderman put it, they were "drifting around the flanks of the position from the slopes to the south, which was a good sign that the Americans were coming forward." He thought he heard Chauchats. From the slope above the position cries of enemy wounded testified to rifle fire from outside the pocket. There was a burst of fire off in the forest to the right, and the Lost Battalion men, wrote the author of a history of the 307th Regiment, "looked at each other as they lay, weak with hunger, among their delirious wounded and their sun-scorched dead, and they questioned each other with the look."[13] Then, through the twilight, a company of American infantry moved in on them, Company B, Lieutenant Frederick A. Tillman commanding, followed by two other companies.

McMurtry remembered that it was 6:45 or 7:00 when a man appeared at the funkhole of Major Whittlesey and said an officer with a patrol had come in on the right and desired to see the commanding officer. Whittlesey said, "I will go up and see just what this is." After he had been gone ten minutes McMurtry followed and found him in conversation with Tillman and "it was an actual fact that we were relieved."[14]

The 307th came in with food. One of the first soldiers walked in with cans of corned beef tied to his bayonet. The companies had sixty cans, and the relieved men counted out the cans and distributed the contents by the spoonful, to be fair.

The relieving companies posted the sides of the pocket, and that night the men of the Lost Battalion slept soundly, in the knowledge that they were safe.

The Lost Battalion—those men who were able to walk out after relief came.
(National Archives)

Major Charles W. Whittlesey.
(National Archives)

**Captain (here Major) Charles
G. McMurtry in 1919, upon
the Seventy-seventh Division's
return to the United States.**
(National Archives)

Major General Robert Alexander in his office dugout in the Argonne Forest. (National Archives)

The dugout from the outside.
(National Archives)

Brigadier General Evan M. Johnson.
(National Archives)

The "pocket" where some five hundred men from two battalions of the 308th Regiment, Seventy-seventh Division, fought off attacking German forces for five days, October 2–7, 1918. (National Archives)

34664

Major General (here Lieutenant General) Hunter Liggett, commander of I Corps, who sought to take out German artillery batteries near Châtel-Chéhéry and relieve the Lost Battalion by threatening the German forces in the Argonne. (National Archives)

Cher Ami, the carrier pigeon released by Major Whittlesey on October 4, 1918. (National Archives)

General John J. Pershing.
(National Archives)

six Aftermath

The aftermath of the experience of the Lost Battalion in the Argonne was at once prosaic and, in its larger dimensions, inspirational.

The next morning, October 8, the former pocket was alive with vehicles and troops as headquarters sections of the Seventy-seventh brought everything they could for the men who had followed their orders and advanced to the division goal without regard to flanks or casualties. General Alexander himself came up and shook Whittlesey's hand, delighted he had met a man who, he believed, was the sort that made the U.S. Army what it had been over the years, a group of soldiers that reached back to Washington's men in 1775, upon whom had fallen the burden of protecting the nation in a time of peril.

The work of the division continued, which was the taking of Grandpré at the top of the bend of the Aire, the town built around an old fortress that the Germans had turned into a new one. In the next days the Seventy-seventh by a large effort—its regiments had been depleted before Whittlesey went into the pocket and were now more so, even with the addition of untrained replacements—managed to take part of the town before October 16, when it relinquished its subsector, now out of the Argonne, to the Seventy-eighth Division.

In First Army the task of taking the entire Meuse-Argonne, all the way to Sedan, remained. Relief of the Lost Battalion had been a sort of apostrophe, a punctuation mark, in the midst of that task.

But the Lost Battalion made a far more important contribution than anything it represented or accomplished in the Meuse-Argonne.

This was its effect on national morale in the years ahead, in the 1920s and 1930s and the initially dark days and months after Pearl Harbor in the early 1940s. The story of the Lost Battalion kept alive the idea of courage. In 1918 the newspaper press seized upon the plight of the trapped battalions in the Argonne, exaggerating and otherwise confusing what had happened, and would do more of the same after the men of the Seventy-seventh came home. In 1919 there was a parade; the entire division, including Whittlesey's survivors, marched up Fifth Avenue in triumph. The sight was impressive: thousands of men in ranks as far as the eye could see, with their brigade and regimental flags flying, their uniforms immaculate, everything in order.

Subsequently, courage almost was lost in a national revulsion against war in any form, as the notion became more widespread that war was fundamentally wrong. Pearl Harbor was such a shock, unbelievable, raising the question of whether the nation faced defeat. Here the example of the Lost Battalion helped bring the country through. Together with what happened at the Alamo and the Little Big Horn, the Lost Battalion stood for courage, defiance in the face of odds, willingness to fight when others might have given up. It stood for what Pershing and Alexander wanted, even if they could not always obtain it, for whatever reasons, good and bad. The division furnished one of the classic examples of courage, of what that priceless quality could bring out in the behavior of a group of apparently very ordinary Americans.

1

On the morning after relief the ridge south of the Charlevaux valley and the valley itself offered a scene resembling a hospital parking lot or a highway rest area, filled with ambulances, trucks, and staff cars. No Germans were to be seen or heard, anywhere in the vicinity, so it was safe enough to bring in all the vehicles. When the 307th's relieving companies came into the area they saw the Germans moving out and could have pursued them but did not. They had been exerting themselves, trying to find a break in the line and get through, and were not in a mood for more exercise. It was dusk, turning into dark, and not a good time to chase Germans. The 307th let them move to the north to, as it turned out, the Kriemhilde Stellung.

On the afternoon of Tuesday, October 8, at 3:00 p.m., the men of the besieged force who were able walked out, led by their major. Initially the plan was that they would go to a place below known as the Dépôt de Machines, but General Alexander wanted them back at headquarters where they could bathe and delouse and get new uniforms, and perhaps also meet the newspapermen who were swarming.

A question arose as to how many men had gone in, and how many of those survived, and the answer never was clear. An estimate made within the Seventy-seventh Division in March–April 1919, before the division went home, was that 419 men including Company K went into the pocket. Captain Kerr Rainsford of the 307th said 600 had gone in. Holderman wrote that the combined force including K numbered 700. Survivors were similarly difficult to count. General Drum's papers said there were 128 from the First Battalion of the 308th and 256 from the Second, 33 from Company K of the 307th, and 21 from the 306th Machine Gun Battalion, for a total of 438. The usually accepted number for the men who walked out, and there may well have been a count at the time, was 194. Rainsford said that half the force survived without serious wounds. He calculated this based on the survivors of Company K of his regiment, figuring that 86 went in (Holderman, who took them in, said the number was 80, while the 1919 estimate was 98) and 43 walked out. According to Drum's papers the men seriously wounded or exhausted who had to be taken out numbered 144. The estimate within the division early in 1919 was 156. In 1932 a hospital list turned up, with the names and serial numbers of men who could not walk out, and it totaled 202. The estimate of 1919 for dead or missing was 69.

An exact roster of the men in the Lost Battalion is probably impossible, beyond the list of 1919 and the hospital list of 1932 (see Appendix Three). In subsequent years innumerable men told their relatives, or the relatives believed such had been the case, that they had been in the Lost Battalion. The list of walk-ins, walk-outs, carried-outs, and dead or missing came to resemble the inflated passenger list for the *Mayflower.*

Similarly, the numbers of surrounding Germans never became clear. Wellmann wrote that the Americans outnumbered his own men. Prinz, writer of the surrender note, interviewed after the war, said that the force behind the Americans numbered 125. Colonel Beattie, the special forces officer of years later who blamed Whittlesey for junior officer tactics, thought the German force small. This could have been the case. It was well known that a few machine-gun nests, fewer in prepared positions, could stop far more men than they, the gunners, possessed. It was true that the German force was not just Huenicken's regiment. Men joined and left the enemy force if so inclined; in the dense forest it was possible to be present or absent. The end of the war was close, little more than a month away, and German forces at the front were beginning to straggle. There was increasing illness; influenza struck the German Army months before the U.S. Army. (It affected the AEF mostly after the war, brought over by last-minute levies from the United States. At the American front the diseases were dysentery and diphtheria.)

The men of the Lost Battalion thought there was a sizable force against them. At one juncture two hundred enemy soldiers reportedly passed around to the south of the pocket. Holderman said the Lost Battalion was "many times outnumbered." Captain Hurley E. Fuller of the American Battle Monuments Commission, who published an article on the Lost Battalion in the *Infantry Journal* in 1926, described the German force as "vastly superior." He may have meant in weapons, but his remark otherwise agreed with the comments of Holderman and other survivors.[1]

Considering the achievement of the Lost Battalion, it is of interest, and in a sense amusing, that among senior officers of the division there was little hesitation in taking credit. With as much modesty as he could muster, which was not much, General Alexander nominated himself. He might have carried off his claim, but after his division got into Grandpré he began talking about his successes there, which was too much—the Seventy-seventh barely took a street in Grandpré, and taking the entire town including the hinterland took another ten days for the Seventy-seventh's successor, the Seventy-eighth Division. General Liggett thereafter tended not to believe anything Alexander said. Influencing Liggett, riding with him in the general's staff car, was the lawyer-turned-major (eventually lieutenant colonel) Stackpole, who disliked Alexander. After the war, early in 1919, the generals of First Army under the then lieutenant general, Liggett, held a series of seminar-like lectures at which the attending generals listened to each other's accomplishments, and

Alexander got into a tangle with Liggett over Grandpré that did his pretensions about any subject no good. So Alexander's claim to be the reliever of the Lost Battalion did not add anything to his laurels.

Brigadier General Johnson made his own claim to being the liberator of Whittlesey's men, as one might have expected. He may have done it to counter Alexander. There had been a moment, when Houghton's men were breaking through, at 2:00 p.m. on October 7, when Johnson felt kindly toward the division commander and was willing to excuse him of bad temper. The moment passed. Even after Alexander gave Johnson some credit for Grandpré and recommended him for major general, Johnson bit the hand that fed him and asked for relief from the Seventy-seventh. He was willing to repeat a statement he had made earlier of how his men accomplished the relief. In 1921 when writing Pershing he put it brightly: "I began to push my men forward so that on the afternoon [evening] of the 7th, the lost battalion was rescued." He pushed the point: "These are the actual facts."[2]

Even Brigadier General McCloskey, probably the author of, certainly the responsible officer for, the barrage of October 4 that shelled the men in the pocket, took credit for saving the men. His claim was a strange one, but he made it, in the course of a contention about La Palette Pavillon to the left of the pocket.

> Between 5-H and 8-H [October 7] a concentration of all the Divisional Artillery was laid on La Palette trench to support a combined Franco-American attack on the German positions to relieve Major Whittlesey's battalion. The attack was not successful, but the artillery fire caused such losses to the enemy in men and material as to compel his withdrawal on the night of 7–8. The results of this fire were later inspected more carefully than any other part of the entire operation to ascertain the accuracy of our fire, because a report was published that the fire was short. A careful investigation was made by the Artillery Brigade Commander, by the Division and Corps Inspectors and the report was found to be without foundation.[3]

General Liggett, who did everything he could to help the Lost Battalion, with the ending of the enfilade from Châtel-Chéhéry being his primary goal in sending up the Eighty-second Division's brigade, never took credit. That was not his way; like Whittlesey, Liggett was not merely laconic but also careful never to claim too much. A member of his staff saved the stub of a pencil that Liggett gave to his chief of staff, Craig, with a piece of paper on which the general had written that the pencil was the one he used to save the Lost Battalion. He may have done this without thought, or believed for a moment that the stub had done the work. Nothing further was heard of his saving the men. Pencil and paper, his only testimony, are in a file in the Military History Institute at Carlisle.[4]

The man who did save the Lost Battalion was Summerall, who never laid claim, probably because it was not he who paid the price but the seven thousand men of his division who died or were wounded. Casualties in the First Division during its advance to Fléville and afterward to the top of the Montrefagne and elsewhere along its line were huge, larger than those of any other attack division in the Meuse-Argonne, even those of the Thirty-fifth Division that did itself in with poor strategy and no tactics and such loose control by its division commander that all units of size passed out of his control.

The men of the Seventy-seventh came home to their parade and mustered out. For a year and more, stories about the Lost Battalion appeared, published in the *New York Times* and elsewhere, especially in the *Los Angeles Times* because after the Oise-Aisne offensive the division received replacements from California.

On November 11, 1921, at Arlington National Cemetery in Washington, a ceremony was held to mark the entombment of the Unknown Soldier, an event that fascinated the nation. It was featured in broadcasts on the new medium of radio, which had "come in" a year or two before. At Arlington the new president of the United States, Warren G. Harding, spoke of the nation's trials in the World War. Present were generals and other officers. In a place of honor were holders of the Congressional Medal, including three officers of the Lost Battalion, Whittlesey, McMurtry, and Holderman.

During the ceremony the three medalists sat together, and Whittlesey made few comments to his fellow medal winners during the entombment and pageantry. The three men sat with a gallant group. It included the Tennessee sharpshooter, Alvin York, who had killed dozens of Germans. Present also was a Kentuckian, a member of the Fifth Division, a Regular soldier made a lieutenant during the war, Samuel Woodfill. Commander of a company stopped by echeloned machine guns, knowing his men were inexperienced, Woodfill went forward with a rifle and pistol and looked for black squares—blankets that German machine gunners hung over the muzzles of their guns to mask the guns' flashes. When he saw a square, smoke curling in front of it, he had his quarry and fired point-blank just below the square, killing gunner after gunner, whereupon he moved to the next square. In a fight at the end he killed a German with a pickax he found in a trench, braining the German. It may be that sitting with such killers as York and Woodfill bothered Whittlesey, inspiring him to say little or nothing, just look ahead.

2

And so, in the years after October 2–7, 1918, in the glow (or was it for Whittlesey a glare?) of what had happened, the years began to pass. As one might have expected, the major, who was a reflective man, was the first to separate himself from the experience, committing suicide within days after the ceremonies at Arlington.

Born in New England, like so many others from his region Whittlesey had been drawn elsewhere, in his case to New York. There he was in partnership in a general law firm for ten years before the war. After his return he expressed interest in banking law and joined the firm of White and Case, at 14 Wall Street. He was not a partner but would have become one. He possessed the best credentials, having attended Williams College and Harvard Law School. His work was eminently satisfactory.

A New Englander to the core, he had a streak of repression in his personality. He was quiet, controlled, and more than a little resembled the prototypical New Englander of his generation, the president of the United States in 1923–1929, Calvin Coolidge. But whereas Coolidge early in a career as a lawyer in Northampton, Massachusetts, had espied the prettiest girl in town, Grace Goodhue, and married her, Whittlesey partook of confirmed bachelorhood. A friend of Whittlesey's later testified that he never had heard the colonel (like McMurtry, who was promoted to major, Whittlesey was also promoted, to lieutenant colonel) mention the name of a woman. The night before he died he took a girl to a show, but she was an old friend and there was no special relationship. He lived in a perhaps former townhouse with a group of other single men, including his brother, an arrangement that would have seemed unlikely today for a retired colonel of his reputation, although such restricted living was common for people of the 1920s. There he had friendly but off-hand relations with the other men. Evenings and weekends he was seen in the Williams or Harvard clubs, reading in the library, working on his legal business, or conversing with members.

His health had never been robust. After return from the war he suffered, as did so many veterans, from a touch of gas. The Germans had spread gas in every likely direction, and unless a soldier was alert—or better, experienced in dealing with gas—it was difficult to avoid. Men in Whittlesey's residence remembered that when he awoke in the mornings or during the nights there were fits of coughing; they could hear them through the walls.

After his return to New York Whittlesey was busy, too much so. He was enlisted by a number of organizations, notably the Red Cross. He was chairman of the New York County chapter's drive between Armistice Day and Thanksgiving 1921 to enroll five hundred thousand new members at one dollar apiece. All the while, for months on end, indigent or otherwise suffering soldiers and their relatives besieged him with telephone calls and letters. And he was appearing at celebrations, such as an affair at the Hippodrome the week before his death to honor the presence of Marshal Foch; the colonel sat on the stage, surrounded by legless or armless veterans.

Two or three times a week he attended funerals. One in particular, in which he walked behind the coffin, bothered him. This was of Private John J. Munson, who had gotten out of the first German pocket on September 29, reporting what had happened to the First Battalion. After the war he enlisted in the Regular Army; stationed at Governors Island he disappeared, reappearing in Bellevue Hospital, where he died of consumption, apparently induced by being gassed during the war. For three days his body lay unclaimed in the city morgue. The tragic affair much affected Whittlesey.

He hardly ever spoke of the war, even with friends, but sometimes related a story from the days of the Lost Battalion in which he had seen a man wounded and was concerned about him. That night the two were in a funkhole together. Whittlesey slept fitfully and awoke in the middle of the night to find his cheek pressing against that of the wounded man, cold in death.

After Thanksgiving Whittlesey took ship on a United Fruit Company steamer, a combination passenger vessel and fruit carrier, the *Toloa.*[5] He told friends at the firm he was going for the weekend to visit relatives. He had visited his parents in Pittsfield, Massachusetts, the weekend before. Just prior to leaving he wrote a one-page will, which he dictated to a stenographer at the firm and had witnessed, but the people who knew this drew nothing from it, as lawyers were always revising their wills. In it he gave one of his decorations to a friend, and to Captain (by then Major) McMurtry he left the original of the German surrender note of October 7, which he had kept. (After the war he had been put in touch with the former Lieutenant Prinz, then working for the American occupation in Koblenz, and told Prinz over the telephone—he himself was in a hospital—that if Prinz ever came to New York he would be glad to see him.) The rest of his possessions, as set out in the will, he left to his ailing mother. His savings were sizable; although less than $10,000, the sum was worth fifteen or twenty times that much in the dollars of later years.

The details of his disappearance on Saturday evening, November 28, 1921, were related in the *New York Times.* The last person to speak with him was a Mr. Maloret of Puerto Rico who had a business in Havana. Whittlesey and Maloret, who had a connection with the AEF in Paris during the war, sat in the smoking room of the steamer, talking a little about the war. They had a drink. The colonel got up abruptly at 11:15, said something about going to his room, and walked out.

No trace of Whittlesey was found, and it could only be assumed that he jumped over the rail. It was cloudy that night, and a fair number of people were on deck, standing around. No one saw him after he left the smoking room. Maloret did not see him the next day, Sunday, and on Monday morning asked the purser about him. He and the purser went to Whittlesey's stateroom and found the door unlocked. They summoned the assistant chief steward and entered, to find the bed unused—the steamer had left New York on Saturday morning. Scattered around were nine letters, one addressed to the ship's captain, Farquahar Grant, the others to friends, all but Grant's written on stationery not available on the ship.

Captain Grant sent a wireless to Whittlesey's former law partner and executor, John B. Pruyn, as the colonel asked him to. The ship arrived in Havana late, by twelve hours. Without telling the passengers, save two or three, the captain had retraced part of his passage in search of a body but found nothing.

The colonel's death was not much of a mystery but never was completely resolved. In his note to Captain Grant he referred to "yesterday," Saturday, which virtually was assurance that he had died early Sunday.

The other survivors of the Lost Battalion, notably the two other winners of the Congressional Medal, McMurtry and Holderman, lived many years afterward, and one may be sure the death of their major was a part of their daily lives, never forgotten. The two surviving medal holders watched the rest of the 1920s go by, a prosperous time, and its turn into the depression-ridden 1930s with its ups and downs, mostly downs, and the coming and course of another war, in which they could have no part, for they were too old.

Holderman was the second of the Lost Battalion's leaders to take his departure, in the (for Whittlesey it would have been) far-off year of 1953, during the presidency of Eisenhower, whose reputation came from World War II and who during World War I had remained a lieutenant colonel of tanks, never leaving the tank cantonment near Gettysburg. Holderman had passed virtually into obscurity. For a while he remained in the army as a Regular, and in 1924–1925 he attended the Infantry School, where he wrote on the Lost Battalion. But apparently the army of that time, despite his extraordinary record, saw no future for him. Or California beckoned. In 1926 he chose to head the State Veterans Home, wherein he died of a heart attack, on September 3, 1953.[6]

A few years later, on November 22, 1958, at age eighty-two, it was the turn of McMurtry. After his war he had returned to New York and prospered in his role of stockbroker, associated with his own firm of Benjamin and McMurtry. Born in Pittsburgh, he had prepared at St. Mark's school before attending Harvard. His clubs were the Racquet and Tennis, the Brook, Knickerbocker, and Harvard. In 1933 he received perpetual membership in the New York Society of Military and Naval Officers of the World War. He retired in 1938. His addresses were Bar Harbor, Maine, and 610 Park Avenue.[7] In September of the year he died, he was host at the Shelburne Hotel of a reunion of the Lost Battalion. Forty-six of the 114 then survivors were in attendance.

By this time the two generals of the Seventy-seventh Division whose orders affected the Lost Battalion had long since died. Alexander retired in 1927, having spent forty-one years in the army. After the war he dropped in rank to colonel, and then in 1921 rose to brigadier. Just before retirement he advanced back to major general. After retirement he took up residence in Tacoma, Washington, then in La Jolla, California. In October 1941 he moved to New York a few weeks before going into the hospital for his last illness. General Johnson in 1919 had become military attaché in Rome, where he was a social figure in the capital because of his knowledge of Italian. He died in Paris in 1923.[8]

In the 1960s and 1970s most of the remaining veterans of World War I passed on. The army had numbered four million, half of the men reaching the battlefield in France. A few veterans, not many, survived into the 1990s. By the turn of the century they were a handful, all centenarians, too old to remember much of what happened during the war of their time, including the story of the Lost Battalion.

appendix one

General Johnson's Protest

General Johnson telephoned the following to Col. Hannay
at 4:00 p.m. on October 2, 1918.

The attack was made as directed. In the 307th the center was held
up by barbed wire, machine guns, hand grenades and infantry. The
right was turning gradually around the flank. The left company,
Capt. Rainsford, had passed by the left of the wire and captured 16
prisoners. At 4 p.m. this message just received from Stacey of the
308th—that his advance elements are on a line 276 and pushing forward. They have captured two machine guns and passed one abandoned machine gun, and captured 28 prisoners, one of which is a
lieutenant. This makes a total of 42 prisoners and two machine guns.
There is a great deal of machine gun fire to the front and flanks—all
around. This is decreasing at present. The 308th is almost to his objective. The 307th is held up in the center by machine guns and
barbed wire 30 feet deep and is at present working around the
flanks to take the Boche in the rear. That was the condition at 2:30.
I do not know the exact conditions at this moment.

I wish you would state this to the General, Hannay—just say this
to him. He told me that if I could not do the work he would get
someone that could. Just say this to him, Hannay. I want you to tell
him just the conditions which I know to be a fact. On my left the
French are fighting on a line in the rear of my troops. I know this from
a Corps observer who has just left them. On my right, the 153rd

Brigade is on a line 75.5. This brigade is and has been away ahead of anything on my right or left. If he will look at the map he will see that relatively the French should be on a line 278, but actually they are back of my line, and that the 153rd should be on a line 277, but they are also to my rear. These elements are not only relatively, but actually behind my troops. I want him to understand absolutely these conditions. The information about the French was given me by a Corps observer who has just left this office and I know what I am talking about. No, this is not a matter of congratulations. I just want him to know absolutely the facts. Well, I am much obliged to you Hannay, but I am, have been and will continue to do my duty to the best of my ability and any time he finds that I am not doing this, he is perfectly free to say so and relieve me.[1]

appendix two

General Johnson's Request for Relief

Headquarters 154th Inf. Brigade,
American E. F., Oct. 7th, 1918.

From: The Commanding General
To: The Commanding General 77th Division, American E. F.
Subject: Further Use of 154th Inf. Brigade in Action.

1. I desire to submit for your consideration and if necessary, for the consideration of higher authority, the impropriety of using this brigade, particularly the 308th Infantry, for further aggressive action in its present condition, against the enemy.

Since September 26th 1918, the troops have been almost daily marching and attacking the enemy, through a trackless jungle, for the first 5 or 6 days without overcoats or blankets, sleeping in cold and rain when they slept, and with an insufficient supply of rations, due to the fact that as before stated, there were no trails open—these had to be cut—and the only way of getting food and ammunition forward was by bearers. Under these conditions a proper issue of food was not possible, and it was impossible to give them hot food particularly since no solidified alcohol or George Washington coffee was available for issue.

This brigade was brought from the Aisne, where for 13 days it had been engaged in action against the enemy in the advance from the Vesle, and reached this place after 5 days marching or traveling in camions and being at once put in line of battle. Prior to this time, it was on the Vesle for about 20 days, where it was under constant fire and where it was engaged in a number of minor operations. The day before it entered into the present battle, there were transferred to it approximately 2000 untrained soldiers from the Depot, the majority of whom had never fired a rifle, thrown a hand grenade, and were entirely ignorant of the elements of military training and of discipline. It will be readily understood that under these conditions the work which has been done has been most arduous, and while the losses have not been excessive—I estimate them to be approximately 2000 killed and wounded—the strain and fatigue which the men have endured has been such that at the present moment they are absolutely unfit for further aggressive action, and I may add, they are unfit to resist an attack of the enemy.

On the afternoon of October 5 and this morning, I personally went to the front and assumed command of that part of the 308th Inf., which was engaged in an attempt to drive the enemy from the entrenched position which he occupies, with a view of relieving the advanced elements of my brigade—parts of 7 companies approximating 240 men—now cut off in the front. On the 5th, the Division Commander directed me to proceed forward and see that the attack as ordered was properly launched. This morning, I did this because I believe that my presence was necessary, and I went further than this and as stated I practically took command of both actions, owing to the fact that the regimental commander was a captain—an intelligent but inexperienced officer, and I felt that by my presence I might put heart into my troops, whom I have commanded for over a year, and that by my professional knowledge I might gain greater results than could otherwise be accomplished. At all times I was within 75 to 300 yards of the actual firing line and practically the same distance from the enemy's trenches, so when I say that these men are not fit to be sent against the enemy, I speak not from any distant, but an immediate, viewpoint. They went without complaint and willingly, but their physical condition was such that it precludes the possibility of success.

This morning the attack was made in conjunction with the French on the left, who were stopped on a line short of ours and who retired before I withdrew my troops—(I withdrew them in accordance with orders). I am now ordered with these same troops to prepare for further aggressive action. I shall, of course, comply with my orders, but I wish to place before the Division Commander and if as stated, it is necessary, request that this communication be forwarded to the Corps Commander, for consideration as to the propriety of such action.

I may state as indicating the results of these two attacks that the force which was immediately engaged October 5th consisted of 7 officers and 443 men. Of these, so far as can be determined, 30 men were killed, two officers and 58 men were wounded and 23 men were missing, a total killed, wounded and missing of 2 officers and 111 men, or approximately 25 percent of the command. In the attack today, the force which actually participated as first line and support, was approximately 500 men. When I left the front and had given orders to withdraw my command [illegible] wounded, it was stated, had been brought in. The number of killed and other wounded I do not know, but these figures will show that the attack was strongly resisted—the resistance being made by infantry, machine guns, high explosives, hand grenades, etc. The French also, it was stated to me by their Liaison Officer, suffered very heavily and said it was impossible to advance further, and therefore retired.

[signed] Evan M. Johnson
Brigadier General NA.
Commanding.[1]

appendix three
Roster of the Lost Battalion

At long last it seems possible to reconstitute a fairly accurate roster of the men in the Lost Battalion, by combining two lists and comparing the result with names in accounts of annual reunions of survivors. In March–April 1919, survivors of the companies of the 308th Regiment and of Company K of the 307th, under guidance of their officers, produced a tentative roster, published in L. Wardlaw Miles, *History of the 308th Infantry: 1917–1919* (New York: Putnam's, 1927). Admittedly it had its problems. The officers asked the men to recall individuals who had died, a procedure that could not account for those killed outside the pocket, seeking to find food or to escape. There was a tendency for men to say they had been in the pocket with Major Whittlesey when they belonged to companies that had been trying to join Whittlesey but had failed to do so.

The largest problem was with hospitalized men who did not return to the Seventy-seventh Division. Survivors did not know what happened to them. Fortunately there is a second list, discovered in 1932, a triage, or hospital, list of 202 men who because of wounds or exhaustion were unable to walk out on the afternoon of October 8. The list includes army serial numbers, ranks, and companies. It is in the National Archives in College Park, Maryland.[1] The triage list is handwritten, and the clerk sometimes employed the old-fashioned small *e* that looks like a capital letter but also used something close to an *i* to represent an *e*. He had trouble with names, perhaps unable to find identification tags on wounded men. The triage list

94

nonetheless adds many names to the list of 1919. These two lists, combined, have been checked with available accounts of annual reunions of the Lost Battalion held in New York in 1955, 1957, and 1958. The minutes include names of those present, messages from individuals unable to attend, and names of survivors who had died since the last meeting.

The list that follows includes as much information as is available from these sources for each man.

Adams, Charles, private, Company K, 307th Infantry
Ahlstedt, Reuben H., private, runner, Second Battalion, 308th
    Infantry, wounded
Albis, Stanislaus, private, Company B, 308th Infantry, wounded
Altiera, Samuel A., private, Company K, 307th Infantry
Amatette, Bart, private, Company B, 308th Infantry
Anastasia, Anthony, private, scout, Second Battalion, 308th Infantry
Anderson, Carl A., private, Company K, 307th Infantry
Anderson, Gus, private, Company K, 307th Infantry, killed
Anderson, Herman G., sergeant, Company A, 308th Infantry
Andrews, Paul F., private, Company G, 308th Infantry, killed
Armstrong, William W., private, Company C, 308th Infantry
Arnold, Harold, private, scout, Second Battalion, 308th Infantry,
    killed

Bachato, Dante, private, Company M, 308th Infantry
Baker, David H., private, Company B, 308th Infantry, wounded
Baker, Edward, private, Company K, 307th Infantry, wounded
Baldwin, Frederick W., sergeant, Company E, 308th Infantry
Baldwin, Joseph K., corporal, Company C, 308th Infantry
Baldwin, Walter J., corporal, headquarters, First Battalion, 308th
    Infantry
Bang, John, private, Company K, 307th Infantry, killed
Barnes, David L., private, headquarters, First Battalion, 308th
    Infantry
Baskin, Louis, private, Company C, 308th Infantry
Becker, Gustave, private, Company C, 306th Machine Gun
    Battalion, killed
Becker, Martin, corporal, Company D, 306th Machine Gun
    Battalion, killed

Bedrna, William, private, scout, Second Battalion, 308th Infantry
Beeson, Leonard R., private, Company K, 307th Infantry, wounded
Begley, William A., private, Company G, 308th Infantry, killed
Bejnarowicz, Joseph, corporal, Company C, 308th Infantry
Belsky, Victor, private, Company A, 308th Infantry
Bendheim, Lionel, sergeant, Company C, 308th Infantry, wounded
Benedetto, Igro, private, Company C, 308th Infantry
Benson, Arthur E., private, Company C, 308th Infantry
Bent, Elmer E., private, Company H, 308th Infantry
Berg, Louis, private, Company K, 307th Infantry
Beriev, Floyd, private, Company K, 307th Infantry, wounded
Beske, Arthur A., private, Company B, 308th Infantry, killed
Bickmore, Harry, private, Company B, 308th Infantry
Bivalace, Giovanni, private, Company K, 307th Infantry, wounded
Blackburn, Raymond, sergeant, Company C, 308th Infantry
Blanchard, Alonso D., corporal, Company K, 307th Infantry
Blomseth, Ludwig, private, Company G, 308th Infantry
Boden, John, private, Company G, 308th Infantry, killed
Bonaventura, Pistoria, private, Company E, 308th Infantry
Botelle, George, private, Company C, 308th Infantry, wounded
Bowden, John, corporal, Company H, 308th Infantry, wounded
Bowers, Bert L., private, Company K, 307th Infantry, wounded
Bradford, Robert F., corporal, Company K, 307th Infantry
Bradshaw, Stanley O., private, Company B, 308th Infantry
Bragg, James W., private, medical detachment, First and Second
    Battalions, 308th Infantry
Braudel, George A., private, headquarters, First Battalion, 308th
    Regiment
Brennan, George H., private, Company D, 306th Machine Gun
    Battalion
Brennen, Harold, private, Company E, 308th Infantry
Brennen, Thomas, corporal, Company C, 308th Infantry
Brew, William F., private, Company K, 307th Infantry, wounded
Brice, James E., private, Company E, 308th Infantry
Bringham, Victor L., private, Company K, 307th Infantry, wounded
Brinkoma, Ralph, private, Company K, 307th Infantry, wounded
Brody, Erving, private, Company B, 308th Infantry
Bronson, Emery, private, Company B, 308th Infantry, wounded
Brown, Clifford R., private, Company C, 308th Infantry

Brown, Edwin C., sergeant, Company H, 308th Infantry, wounded
Brown, Gilbert, private, Company K, 307th Infantry, missing
Bruton, James, private, Company G, 308th Infantry, killed
Bueskins, Herbert, private, Company K, 307th Infantry, wounded
Buhler, Fred, second lieutenant, Company G, 308th Infantry, wounded
Burns, William C., private, Company H, 308th Infantry
Buth, Henry C., private, Company H, 308th Infantry, killed

Cadeux, Henry J., private, Company B, 308th Infantry, wounded
Caldwell, Louis B., private, Company H, 308th Infantry
Cameron, John, private, Company K, 307th Infantry
Cappiello, Savino, Company C, 308th Infantry
Carnebucci, Catino, private, Company C, 308th Infantry, killed
Carroll, James B., sergeant, Company K, 307th Infantry
Cassidy, Henry, private, Company C, 308th Infantry, wounded
Castrogiovanna, Joseph, private, Company C, 308th Infantry, killed
Cathcart, Joseph E., private, Company H, 308th Infantry
Cathcart, Noble, private, Company K, 307th Infantry
Cavanaugh, William, private, Company C, 308th Infantry
Cavello, Thomas, private, Company H, 308th Infantry, killed
Cella, Innocenzo, private, Company A, 308th Infantry
Cepeglia, Philip, private, Company C, 308th Infantry
Chamberlain, James, private, Company K, 307th Infantry
Chambers, Joseph, private, Company H, 308th Infantry, wounded
Chandler, Charles, private, Company B, 308th Infantry
Charlesworth, Percy, private, Company C, 308th Infantry, wounded
Chavelle, Charles H., private, Company B, 308th Infantry, wounded
Chinn, Henry, private, Company H, 308th Infantry, killed
Chiswell, George H., Company E, 308th Infantry, wounded
Christ, Charles F., private, Company K, 307th Infantry
Christensen, Hans, private, Company K, 307th, Infantry
Christenson, Fred, private, Company E, 308th Infantry
Christenson, Philip, private, Company K, 307th Infantry
Christian, Robert E., private, Company H, 308th Infantry, killed
Christopher, Joseph, private, Company K, 307th Infantry, wounded
Chupp, Emmon, private, runner, Second Battalion, 308th Infantry, wounded
Church, Roscoe G., private, Company K, 307th Infantry, killed

Clark, Raymond O., private, Company H, 308th Infantry, killed
Clarke, Nathan, private, Company D, 306th Machine Gun Battalion, killed
Clay, Thomas H., private, Company H, 308th Infantry, wounded
Clemons, Melvin E., private, Company G, 308th Infantry
Coatney, Arthur F., private, Company H, 308th Infantry, wounded
Coe, Richard R., private, Company H, 308th Infantry, wounded
Cohen, Morris, private, Company D, 306th Machine Gun Battalion, wounded
Colan, James, corporal, Company G, 308th Infantry, wounded
Colasacco, John G., sergeant, Company C, 308th Infantry
Cole, Harvey R., private, Company K, 307th Infantry, killed
Collins, John, private, Company A, 308th Infantry, wounded
Cologers, Lamonaco, private, Company F, 308th Infantry
Condon, James T., private, Company C, 308th Infantry
Conneally, John, private, Company G, 308th Infantry
Connelly, John, private, Company E, 308th Infantry, wounded
Connelly, Timothy, private, Company K, 307th Infantry
Connolly, Patrick, private, Company D, 308th Infantry
Conrad, James M., private, Company D, 306th Machine Gun Battalion, killed
Conroy, Francis J., second lieutenant, Company M, 308th Infantry
Coppielo, Savine, private, Company C, 308th Infantry
Copsey, Albert, corporal, Company B, 308th Infantry
Cordell, Thomas F., private, Company B, 308th Infantry
Cornell, Charles B., corporal, Company H, 308th Infantry
Cornell, Henry C., private, 306th Machine Gun Battalion, wounded
Crosby, John, private, Company C, 308th Infantry, wounded
Crotly, Martin J., private, Company D, 306th Machine Gun Battalion, wounded
Crouse, William P., private, Company K, 307th Infantry, killed
Cullen, William J., first lieutenant, Company H, 308th Infantry
Cunningham, Niles F., private, Company C, 308th Infantry
Cummings, Roy, private, Company H, 308th Infantry
Curley, Edward T., private, Company C, 308th Infantry, wounded
Curtin, Thomas, private, Company B, 308th Infantry

Dahlgren, Gus, private, Company G, 308th Infantry, wounded
Damcott, John, private, Company C, 308th Infantry, killed

Damon, Harry P., private, Company H, 308th Infantry
Dayo, Harrison, private, scout, Second Battalion, 308th Infantry
Deaderick, Osro, private, Company G, 308th Infantry
Deahan, James A., sergeant, Company K, 307th Infantry
Delford, George, private, Company E, 308th Infantry
Delgrosso, Frank, private, Company G, 308th Infantry, wounded
Delmont, John, private, scout, Second Battalion, 308th Infantry
Del Sasso, John L., private, Company E, 308th Infantry
Delserone, John, private, Company H, 308th Infantry, wounded
Demmick, Frank C., private, Company D, 306th Machine Gun
    Battalion, killed
Diesil, Louis, private, Company D, 306th Machine Gun Battalion, killed
Digiacomo, Frank, private, Company G, 308th Infantry
Dingledine, E. N., private, Company D, 306th Machine Gun
    Battalion, killed
Disfumo, Pietro, private, Company B, 308th Infantry
Dodd, Robert, private, Company H, 308th Infantry
Doherty, Arthur A., corporal, runner, Second Battalion, 308th
    Infantry, wounded
Domrose, Walter L., Company E, 308th Infantry, missing
Downs, Lee H., private, Company C, 308th Infantry
Drake, Herbert M., private, Company H, 308th Infantry
Drydal, Joseph B., private, Company B, 308th Infantry, killed
Duffy, George W., corporal, Company B, 308th Infantry
Dunham, Ralph G., private, runner, Second Battalion, 308th
    Infantry
Dunnigan, Thomas, private, Company B, 308th Infantry
Duryea, Cecil I., private, Company H, 308th Infantry, wounded

Eager, Sherman W., second lieutenant, Company G, 308th Infantry
Edlund, Hermand, private, Company G, 308th Infantry
Edwards, Lyle J., private, Company H, 308th Infantry
Eggleston, George, private, Company D, 306th Machine Gun
    Battalion
Eichorn, John, private, runner, Second Battalion, 308th Infantry
Ekberg, George, private, Company H, 308th Infantry
Elkin, Gabe, private, Company H, 308th Infantry
Ellbogen, Martin, private, scout, Second Battalion, 308th Infantry,
    wounded

Elliott, Frederick, private, Company G, 308th Infantry, wounded
Engen, Conrad, private, Company H, 308th Infantry, wounded
Englander, George M., bugler, Company G, 308th Infantry, wounded
Erdahl, Olaf, private, Company H, 308th Infantry
Erickson, Alfred E., private, Company H, 308th Infantry, killed
Erickson, Arthur, private, Company G, 308th Infantry
Erickson, Frank G. S., private, Company H, 308th Infantry
Erickson, Henry, private, Company A, 308th Infantry, wounded
Estes, Frank R., private, Company H, 308th Infantry
Etenauer, Albert A., private, Company M, 307th Infantry
Evans, Peter, private, Company H, 308th Infantry, wounded

Fairbanks, Truman P., private, Company G, 308th Infantry, wounded
Fare, John, private, Company K, 307th Infantry, wounded
Farland, Wade, corporal, Company G, 308th Infantry
Farncomb, Harvey, private, Company D, 308th Infantry
Fassett, Ancel E., private, Company H, 308th Infantry, killed
Fassino, Jim, private, Company H, 308th Infantry
Feeney, Francis, private, Company B, 308th Infantry
Fein, Arthur E., private, Company K, 307th Infantry, wounded
Felton, James P., private, Company K, 307th Infantry, wounded
Feuerlicht, Samuel, private, Company C, 308th Infantry, killed
Fitzgerald, Leo, private, Company M, 308th Infantry
Fitzgerald, Peter A., private, Company G, 308th Infantry, wounded
Fitzgerald, William, private, Company D, 308th Infantry
Flack, Earl A., private, Company H, 308th Infantry
Flaming, Henry P., private, Company H, 308th Infantry
Flatney, Brede, private, Company M, 308th Infantry
Flower, Leo A., private, Company C, 306th Machine Gun Battalion
Flynn, John T., private, Company B, 308th Infantry
Flynn, Raymond, Company E, 308th Infantry
Fortunato, Joseph C., private, Company C, 308th Infantry
Foss, private
Francis, William E., private, Company H, 308th Infantry, wounded
Fredette, Frank D. S., private, runner, Second Battalion, 308th
    Infantry
Freeman, Harry, sergeant, Company G, 308th Infantry, wounded
Friel, Joseph, private, Company A, 308th Infantry, killed
Frink, Charles W., private, Company C, 308th Infantry, wounded
Frost, Clarence H., private, Company H, 308th Infantry

Gaedeke, Benjamin F., sergeant major, headquarters, First Battalion, 308th Infantry, killed

Gafanowitz, Robert, private, Company G, 308th Infantry, wounded

Gallagher, Dennis A., private, Company G, 308th Infantry, wounded

Gallob, Hyman, private, Company B, 308th Infantry, killed

Gaupset, Siguard, private, Company E, 308th Infantry, wounded

Geanekos, Agel, private, company B, 308th Infantry

Gehris, John, private, medical detachment, First and Second Battalions, 308th Infantry

Gibbons, Peter, private, Company K, 307th Infantry

Gibson, Herbert B., private, Company H, 308th Infantry, wounded

Giganti, Joseph, private, Company C, 308th Infantry

Gill, Thoma H., private, Company K, 307th Infantry

Gillece, Bernard, corporal, scout, Second Battalion, 308th Infantry

Gilley, George, corporal, Company K, 307th Infantry

Gitchell, Leonard C., private, Company H, 308th Infantry, killed

Gladd, David, private, Company C, 308th Infantry, killed

Glenn, Leonard, private, Company B, 308th Infantry

Goldhorn, Henry W., private, scout, Second Battalion, 308th Infantry

Gorice, Joseph, private, Company H, 308th Infantry

Gould, John A., private, Company B, 308th Infantry

Graham, Charles H., private, Company K, 307th Infantry

Graham, Robert J., sergeant, Company D, 306th Machine Gun Battalion, killed

Grant, LeRoy, private, Company E, 308th Infantry

Greally, Michael, sergeant, Company G, 308th Infantry, killed

Green, Bert M., corporal, Company K, 307th Infantry

Greenfield, Barney, private, Company B, 308th Infantry

Greenwald, Irving W., private, scout, Second Battalion, 308th Infantry

Griffin, Maurice B., first lieutenant, Company H, 308th Infantry, wounded

Griswold, Lester, private, Company C, 308th Infantry, wounded

Gross, Herbert, private, Company E, 308th Infantry

Grossberg, Percy, private, scout, Second Battalion, 308th Infantry

Gudis, Peter C., Company E, 308th Infantry

Habeck, Frank, private, Company E, 308th Infantry, wounded

Hadlow, Rubin, private, Company A, 308th Infantry, wounded

Hagerman, Mark C., sergeant, Company G, 308th Infantry
Hall, Charles E., private, Company B, 308th Infantry
Halligan, William C., private, Company B, 308th Infantry, killed
Halt, John, private, Company B, 308th Infantry
Halverson, Louis
Hamilton, John R., private, runner, Second Battalion, 308th
    Infantry
Hammond, Raymond, private, Company B, 308th Infantry
Hanson, Theodore, private, Company E, 308th Infantry, killed
Hanson, V. E., private, headquarters, First Battalion, 308th Infantry
Hanson, Walter, private, Company B, 308th Infantry
Harch, private, Company D, 306th Machine Gun Battalion
Harkleroad, Lee C., private, Company C, 306th Machine Gun
    Battalion
Harlick, Max, private, Company A, 308th Infantry
Harlin, Albert, private, Company D, First Battalion, 308th Infantry
Harrington, Victor A., second lieutenant, Company E, 308th
    Infantry, wounded and missing
Harris, William, private, Company G, 308th Infantry
Hatch, Boyd, Company K, 307th Infantry
Hatcher, Otto R., private, Company C, 308th Infantry
Hauck, George E., sergeant, Company D, 306th Machine Gun
    Battalion
Hazen, Louis W., private, Company C, 308th Infantry, wounded
Healey, Jeremiah, sergeant, Company G, 308th Infantry, wounded
Hearty, James, private, Company B, 308th Infantry, wounded
Hecker, Arthur J., private, Company H, 308th Infantry
Hedrick, Anthony, private, Company A, 308th Infantry
Helaney, William S., private, Company C, 308th Infantry
Held, Jacob, corporal, Company C, 308th Infantry
Hendrickson, Alfred, private, Company K, 307th Infantry,
    wounded
Hepworth, Clyde, private, Company H, 308th Infantry, wounded
Hermsdorf, Harry J., sergeant, Company B, 308th Infantry
Heuer, Joseph P., sergeant, Company K, 307th Infantry
Hicks, Arthur, private, Company K, 307th Infantry, wounded
Hicks, Stacy M., private, Company C, 308th Infantry
Hiduck, Anthony, private, Company A, 308th Infantry, wounded
Hildenbrand, Carl, private, Company B, 308th Infantry, killed

Hinchman, John, private, Company C, 308th Infantry, killed
Hintz, Clyde C. A., private, Company B, 308th Infantry
Hission, William, private, Company C, 308th Infantry
Hoadley, George, private, Company K, 307th Infantry
Hodge, Chester, private, Company B, 308th Infantry
Hogue, Frank D., private, Company K, 307th Infantry
Holbert, Edward, private, Company H, 308th Infantry
Holden, Wyatt L., private, Company C, 308th Infantry
Holderman, Nelson M., captain, Company K, 307th Infantry,
    wounded
Holen, David, private, Company D, 308th Infantry
Holliday, William M., private, Company B, 308th Infantry, killed
Hollingshead, Lowell R., private, Company H, 308th Infantry
Holt, James M., private, Company D, 306th Machine Gun Battalion
Holt, John, private, Company B, 308th Infantry, wounded
Holzer, William, private, Company G, 308th Infantry, wounded
Honas, Stephen M., private, Company B, 308th Infantry
Hoof, Henry, private, Company D, 308th Infantry
Hover, Sylvester, private, Company B, 308th Infantry, killed
Hudlow, Reuben, private, Company A, 308th Infantry
Huff, George, private, Company K, 307th Infantry
Huntington, Lloyd A., private, Company H, 308th Infantry, wounded
Hyde, Richard W., private, Company H, 308th Infantry, killed

Ignaszewski, Peter, private, Company D, 308th Infantry
Iltz, Henry, private, Company C, 307th Machine Gun Battalion
Indiana, Dominick, private, Company C, 308th Infantry
Ingraham, Theodore, private, scout, Second Battalion, 308th
    Infantry

Jackson, Louis, private, Company K, 307th Infantry
Jacob, William, sergeant, Company C, 308th Infantry
Jacobson, Kittel, private, Company C, 308th Regiment
Jacoby, Leo J., private, Company C, 308th Infantry
Jeffreys, private, Battery D, 305th Field Artillery, missing
Jepson, Earl F., private, Company B, 308th Infantry, killed
Jessman, Clarence, private, Headquarters, First Battalion, 308th
    Infantry
John, Roy E., private, Company A, 308th Infantry

Johnson, Charles, private, Company K, 307th Infantry, killed
Johnson, Grover C., private, Company A, 308th Infantry
Johnson, Louis N., private, Company C, 306th Machine Gun
    Battalion, killed
Johnson, Maurice E., sergeant, Company D, 306th Machine Gun
    Battalion
Johnson, Raymond, private, Company C, 308th Infantry, wounded
Johnson, William, private, Company A, 308th Infantry, killed
Jones, Arthur H., private, Company B, 308th Infantry, killed
Jones, David O., private, Company K, 307th Infantry
Jorgensen, Arthur, private, scout, Second Battalion, 308th Infantry
Jorgenson, Herbert, private, Company G, 308th Infantry, wounded
Joyce, Joseph, private, Company H, 308th Infantry, wounded
Judd, Roland P., private, Company A, 308th Infantry, killed
Judis, Peter C., corporal, Company E, 308th Infantry

Kaempfer, Albert O., private, Company K, 307th Infantry, wounded
Karaluinas, John, private, Company K, 307th Infantry, wounded
Karpinsky, Frank, private, Company B, 308th Infantry, wounded
Karpovich, Joseph
Kaspirovitch, Jacob, private, Company E, 308th Infantry, wounded
Kaufman, Emil, private, Company C, 308th Infantry
Keegan, James A., private, Company B, 308th Infantry
Keenan, Joseph C., corporal, Company D, 306th Machine Gun
    Battalion
Keeney, Jess, private, Company C, 306th Machine Gun Battalion
Keim, George, private, Company C, 308th Infantry
Kelly, Joseph D., private, Company D, 306th Machine Gun
    Battalion, wounded
Kelly, Kennedy K., private, Company A, 308th Infantry, killed
Kelly, Michael, private, scout, Second Battalion, 308th Infantry
Kelmel, William, private, Company K, 307th Infantry
Kempe, Edward, private, headquarters, First Battalion, 308th
    Infantry
Kennedy, Edward A., private, Company D, 306th Machine Gun
    Battalion, wounded
Kennedy, Joseph, corporal, Company G, 308th Infantry
Kiernan, Joseph, private, Company E, 308th Infantry
King, Joseph, private, Company C, 308th Infantry

Kirchner, Gerard, sergeant, Company H, 308th Infantry
Klein, Irving, corporal, Company A, 308th Infantry, wounded
Knabe, William H., private, Company K, 307th Infantry, wounded
Knauss, Daniel M., private, Company H, 308th Infantry
Knettel, John J., private, Company K, 307th Infantry
Knifaund, Otto M., private, Company C, 308th Infantry
Knott, Carlton V., private, Company B, 308th Infantry, killed
Knutson, Carl, private, Company D, 308th Infantry
Koebler, George, private, Company C, 306th Machine Gun Battalion,
    wounded
Kolbe, Charles A., private, Company C, 306th Machine Gun
    Battalion, wounded
Kornelly, Philip, private, Company B, 308th Infantry, wounded
Kosikowski, Stanislaw, private, Company C, 308th Infantry
Kostinen, Frank J., private, Company C, 308th Infantry
Krantz, Walter J., private, Company C, 308th Infantry
Krotoshinsky, Abraham, private, Company K, 307th Infantry

Labounty, Lewis J., private, Company B, 308th Infantry
Laine, Rheinholt N., private, Company B, 308th Infantry
Laird, Alex, private, Company B, 308th Infantry
Lander, Frank N., private, Company C, 308th Infantry
Landers, Patrick J., sergeant, Company H, 308th Infantry
Larkin, Archie F., private, Company C, 308th Infantry
Larney, James F., private, headquarters, 308th Infantry, wounded
Larson, Erik, private, Company C, 308th Infantry
Layman, Ray E., private, Company G, 308th Infantry
Leak, James V., first lieutenant, Company E, 308th Infantry, wounded
    and missing
Leflaer, Len L., private, Company H, 308th Infantry
Lehmeier, Joseph, private, Company K, 307th Infantry
Lekan, Michael, private, Company K, 307th Infantry, killed
Lesley, James E., private, Company H, 308th Infantry
Lesnick, Max, private, Company C, 308th Infantry
Levine, Joseph, private, scout, Second Battalion, 308th Infantry
Lightfoot, Roy H., Company C, 308th Infantry
Lindley, Gilbert, private, Company G, 308th Infantry
Liner, Irving L., private, Company D, 308th Infantry
Lipacher, Isaac, private, Company K, 307th Infantry, wounded

Lipasti, Frank, private, Company K, 307th Infantry, killed
Little, Robert J., private, Company H, 308th Infantry, killed
Lokken, Martin O., private, Company B, 308th Infantry
Lonergan, James E., private, Company D, 306th Machine Gun
    Battalion, wounded
Long, Patrick, private, Company K, 307th Infantry
Lovell, Arthur R., private, Company G, 308th Infantry
Lowman, Cecil, private, Company C, 308th Infantry
Luckett, Henry C., private, Company H, 308th Infantry, killed
Lucy, William J., private, Company H, 308th Infantry
Lukas, Michael J., private, runner, Second Battalion, 308th Infantry
Lund, Ole, private, Company C, 308th Infantry
Lyons, Frank J., private, Company K, 307th Infantry
Lyons, Thomas J., private, Company H, 308th Infantry, killed
Lysen, Chester, private, Company C, 308th Infantry

McArenche, Philip, private, Company E, 308th Infantry
McCabe, John, private, Company C, 308th Infantry
McCallion, John J., private, runner, Second Battalion, 308th
    Infantry
McCarthy, John A., private, Company H, 308th Infantry
McCauley, Jesse J., private, Company G, 308th Infantry
McCoy, Bert C., private, Company A, 308th Infantry, wounded
McCoy, John W., private, Company B, 308th Infantry
McElroy, Joseph, private, Company C, 306th Machine Gun
    Battalion
McFeron, Olin, private, Company C, 308th Infantry
McGowan, Terrence, private, Company B, 308th Infantry
McGowen, Joseph L., private, Company C, 308th Infantry
McGrath, Eugene, private, Company C, 308th Infantry, killed
McJunkins, Jay, private, Company H, 308th Infantry
McMahon, Martin, corporal, Company B, 308th Infantry, wounded
McMurtry, George G., captain, Second Battalion, 308th Infantry,
    wounded
McNearney, John A., private, Company H, 308th Infantry
Macali, Joseph, private, Company B, 308th Infantry, wounded
Macy, David, private, Company A, 308th Infantry
Magnusson, David, private, scout, Second Battalion, 308th Infantry,
    wounded

Mahon, F. W.

Main, Fred T., sergeant, Company C, 308th Infantry

Majgren, Edward, private, Company C, 308th Infantry

Mandell, Fred A., private, Company C, 308th Infantry, wounded

Maney, Patrick, private, Company E, 308th Infantry, wounded

Mann, Sydney C., private, Company H, 308th Infantry

Mannion, Thomas J., private, Company K, 307th Infantry

Manson, Robert, private, Company B, 308th Infantry

Marcali, Joseph, private, Company B, 308th Infantry

Marchelwaki, Stephen, private, Company C, 308th Infantry

Marcus, Samuel, sergeant, Company B, 308th Infantry

Marcy, Leo W., corporal, Company D, 306th Machine Gun Battalion, killed

Mares, Rito, private, Company G, 308th Infantry

Marion, Roy L., private, Company C, 308th Infantry

Marker, O. A., private, Company C, 308th Infantry

Martin, Albert E., private, Company K, 307th Infantry, wounded

Martin, Wayne W., private, Company A, 308th Infantry

Martin, William, private, Company G, 308th Infantry, killed

Materna, Joseph, private, Company K, 307th Infantry

Mathews, Andrew, private, Company H, 308th Infantry

Mathews, Richard W., corporal, Company B, 308th Infantry

Mattano, Joseph, private, 306th Machine Gun Battalion

Mauro, Frank, private, Company H, 308th Infantry, wounded

Mayhew, George, private, Company C, 308th Infantry

Mears, Robert L., private, Company C, 308th Infantry

Medboc, Joseph, private, Company C, 308th Infantry

Mele, Michael, private, Company G, 308th Infantry, wounded

Meltam, Nick, private, Company A, 308th Infantry

Mendenhall, Jesse J., private, Company H, 308th Infantry, killed

Merrill, Victor, private, Company B, 308th Infantry

Merry, Ernest S., corporal, Company E, 308th Infantry, killed

Mersch, Pierre C., private, Company B, 308th Infantry

Mewby, Ernest S., private, Company E, 308th Infantry

Meyerowitz, Robias, private, Company K, 307th Infantry

Miller, Fernnau, private, Company H, 308th Infantry

Miller, Henry, private, Company E, 308th Infantry, killed

Miller, Nathaniel, private, Company G, 308th Infantry, wounded

Miller, Ray T., private, Company B, 308th Infantry

Mimera, Joseph, private, Company B, 308th Infantry
Monan, Robert P., private, Company K, 307th Infantry
Monk, William J., private, Company C, 308th Infantry
Moren, Arnold M., private, Company E, 308th Infantry, wounded
Morgan, Thomas J., private, Company B, 308th Infantry
Morris, Albert, private, Company C, 308th Infantry
Morris, Louis, private, Company B, 308th Infantry, wounded
Morrow, Bert B., sergeant, Company C, 308th Infantry
Munson, Gustave, private, Company H, 308th Infantry, wounded
Murphy, James, sergeant, Company K, 307th Infantry
Murphy, John, private, Company C, 308th Infantry
Murray, Kenneth, private, Company K, 307th Infantry
Murray, Thomas, private, Company K, 307th Infantry
Mynard, Edwin S., sergeant, Company D, 306th Machine Gun
    Battalion

Nauheim, Alfred P., corporal, Company A, 308th Infantry
Nell, John, Company G, 308th Infantry
Nelson, Arthur G., private, scout, Second Battalion, 308th Infantry,
    wounded
Nelson, Olaf
Neptune, Harold B., private, Company H, 308th Infantry, wounded
Nies, George W., private, Company H, 308th Infantry, killed
Nilsen, Olaf, corporal, Company H, 308th Infantry
Noon, Alfred R., second lieutenant, Company C, 306th Machine Gun
    Battalion, killed
Norton, Grant S., private, Company B, 308th Infantry, killed

O'Brien, Lewis, private, Company C, 308th Infantry
O'Connell, James P., corporal, Company D, 306th Machine Gun
    Battalion
Ofstad, Gile, private, Company K, 307th Infantry, wounded
O'Keefe, Thomas C., bugler, Company D, 306th Machine Gun
    Battalion, killed
O'Keeffe, John, private, scout, Second Battalion, 308th Infantry,
    wounded
Oliver, Walter T., private, Company D, 306th Machine Gun
    Battalion, wounded
Olson, Fred, private, Company C, 308th Infantry

Olson, Lars, private, Company C, 308th Infantry
Olstren, Andrew, private, Company K, 307th Infantry
Orlando, Angel, private, Company H, 308th Infantry, wounded
Osborne, Lawrence, sergeant, Company B, 308th Infantry, killed
Ostrovsky, Isadore, private, Company H, 308th Infantry
Oxman, Charles, private, Company C, 308th Infantry

Pagliaro, Benjamin, private, Company G, 308th Infantry
Pardue, Robert M., private, Company E, 308th Infantry
Parker, George W., Company F, 308th Infantry
Patterson, Clarence, private, runner, Second Battalion, 308th
    Infantry
Payne, Andrew, private, Company C, 308th Infantry, wounded
Peabody, Marshall G., second lieutenant, Company D, 306th
    Machine Gun Battalion, killed
Pennington, Joseph R., private, Company E, 308th Infantry, wounded
Perea, Enrique, private, Company H, 308th Infantry
Perrigo, Myron D., private, Company G, 308th Infantry, wounded
Pesetti, Salvatore, private, Company K, 307th Infantry
Peters, Clarence, private, Company B, 308th Infantry
Peterson, Carl H., private
Peterson, Emil A., private, Company H, 308th Infantry, wounded
Peterson, Holger, corporal, Company G, 308th Infantry, killed
Peterson, Hugo E., private, Company B, 308th Infantry
Peterson, Lafayette, private, Company A, 308th Infantry
Peterson, Walter S., private, Company B, 308th Infantry, wounded
Petti, Alfred J., private, scout, Second Battalion, 308th Infantry
Phelps, Jacob C., private, Company K, 307th Infantry, wounded
Picconi, Nicoli, private
Pierson, John L., private, Company K, 307th Infantry
Pinkstone, Charles, private, Company C, 308th Infantry, wounded
Pistoria, Bonaventura, private, Company B, 308th Infantry, wounded
Pollinger, Frank, private, Company G, 308th Infantry, wounded
Pomeroy, Lawrence, private, Company B, 308th Infantry
Pool, Thomas G., first lieutenant, Company K, 307th Infantry,
    wounded
Pope, Calegere, private, Company K, 307th Infantry
Potter, Oscar, private, Company G, 308th Infantry, wounded
Pou, Robert E., Company E, 308th Infantry

Powell, Josephus, private, Company H, 308th Infantry, wounded
Powers, William J., private, headquarters, First Battalion, 308th
Infantry
Probst, Louis M., mechanic, scout, Second Battalion, 308th Infantry
Prusek, Joseph, private, Company K, 307th Infantry
Pugh, Charles J., private, runner, Second Battalion, 308th Infantry
Puniskin, Joseph H., private, Company C, 308th Infantry

Rainwater, Carl A., private, runner, Second Battalion, 308th Infantry
Ratto, Vito, private, Company E, 308th Infantry
Rauchle, Frank, corporal, Company C, 306th Machine Gun Battalion
Rayony, Spiro, private, runner, Second Battalion, 308th Infantry
Rayson, Homer, private, scout, Second Battalion, 308th Infantry, killed
Recko, Jack, private, Company H, 308th Infantry
Rector, Frank C., corporal, Company D, 306th Machine Gun
Battalion
Regan, William, private, Company G, 308th Infantry
Reid, Lauren G., private, Company G, 308th Infantry, killed
Reiger, John, Company B, 308th Infantry, wounded
Renda, John, private, Company H, 308th Infantry, wounded
Revnes, Maurice S., second lieutenant, Company D, 306th Machine
Gun Battalion, wounded
Reynolds, John, private, Company C, 308th Infantry, killed
Rhoads, Solomon E., private, Company H, 308th Infantry
Rice, Chauncey I., corporal, Company D, 306th Machine Gun
Battalion
Richards, Omer, private, headquarters, First Battalion, 308th
Infantry
Richardson, private, Company C, 306th Machine Gun Battalion
Richter, Morris, private, Company C, 308th Infantry
Ridlon, Ernest J., private, Company G, 308th Infantry, wounded
Ritter, Charles, private, Company H, 308th Infantry, wounded
Ritter, Vern, private, Company H, 308th Infantry
Roberts, Benjamin, private, Company K, 307th Infantry, wounded
Roberts, Clarence, Company B, 308th Infantry
Robertson, Arch, private, Company H, 308th Infantry
Rodriguez, Alfred, private, scout, Second Battalion, 308th Infantry
Roesch, Clarence R., sergeant major, headquarters, Second Battalion,
308th Infantry

Rogers, Harry M., second lieutenant, Company B, 308th Infantry, killed

Rommel, Clarence, private, Company E, 308th Infantry

Ronan, Maurice H., private, Company C, 306th Machine Gun Battalion

Rosby, Thornweld, private, Company K, 307th Infantry, wounded

Rose, Sidney, private, Company E, 308th Infantry, wounded

Rosenberg, Samuel, private, Company H, 308th Infantry, killed

Ross, Albert A., private, Company G, 308th Infantry, killed

Rossurn, Haakon A., corporal, Company G, 308th Infantry, wounded

Rousseau, Ernest J., private, headquarters, First Battalion, 308th Infantry

Rowjorny, Spiro, private, Company G, 308th Infantry

Royall, Joseph, private, Company H, 308th Infantry

Rufo, Donato, private, Company G, 308th Infantry

Rugg, Hiram M., private, Company H, 308th Infantry, killed

Rumsey, Wilbert F., private, Company K, 307th Infantry, killed

Ruppe, John, private, scout, Second Battalion, 308th Infantry, killed

Ryan, John F., corporal, Company D, 306th Machine Gun Battalion, killed

Sackman, Julius, sergeant, Company D, 306th Machine Gun Battalion

Sadler, Thomas G., private, Battery D, 308th Field Artillery

St. Cartier, Lucien, private, Company C, 308th Infantry, killed

Sands, Lester T., private, scout, Second Battalion, 308th Infantry

Santillo, Anthony, private, Company D, 306th Machine Gun Battalion, killed

Santini, Giuseppe, private, Company G, 308th Infantry

Scanlon, John H., private, Company D, 306th Machine Gun Battalion, wounded

Schanz, Joseph, private, Company G, 308th Infantry

Schenderline, Joseph, private, Company H, 308th Infantry

Schenck, Gordon L., second lieutenant, Company C, 308th Infantry, killed

Schettino, Lememe, private, Company K, 307th Infantry

Schmidt, John, mechanic, Company G, 308th Infantry, wounded

Schmitz, Joseph J., private, Company D, 306th Machine Gun Battalion, wounded

Schultz, William, private, Company G, 308th Infantry
Schwanbeck, Arthur, private, Company K, 307th Infantry, wounded
Schwartz, Paul A., corporal, Company K, 307th Infantry
Scialdono, Giuseppe, private, Company K, 307th Infantry, wounded
Searfus, Bert, private, Company B, 308th Infantry
Segal, Paul, Company C, 308th Infantry
Seig, Eugene, private, Company G, 308th Infantry
Semenuk, Harry, private, Company C, 308th Infantry
Senter, Henry H., private, Company H, 308th Infantry, wounded
Seyfert, Waldo, private, headquarters, First Battalion, 308th Infantry
Shaffer, Harry L., corporal, Company H, 308th Infantry, wounded
Shepard, Arthur H., Company G, 308th Infantry
Sicherman, Jack, corporal, Company M, 308th Infantry
Silva, Frank, private, Company H, 308th Infantry
Sims, George, corporal, Company K, 307th Infantry
Sirota, Irving, private, medical detachment, First and Second
    Battalions, 308th Infantry
Sketson, Orlander, Company B, 308th Infantry, missing
Slingerland, James E., private, Company G, 308th Infantry
Smith, Sidney, private, Company H, 308th Infantry
Snavely, Charles, private
Sobaszkegicz, Stanley, private, Company H, 308th Infantry, wounded
Solomon, Arthur, private, Company F, 308th Infantry
Spallina, Joseph, private, Company K, 307th Infantry, wounded
Speich, George P., corporal, Company K, 307th Infantry
Spiegel, Isadore, private, Company H, 308th Infantry
Stamboni, Joseph, private, Company D, 306th Machine Gun
    Battalion, wounded
Stanfield, John A., private, Company H, 308th Infantry
Stanley, Lawrence, corporal, Company G, 308th Infantry
Steichen, Albert N., private, Company H, 308th Infantry
Stenger, W., private, Company H, 308th Infantry
Stingle, Frank, private, Company K, 307th Infantry, wounded
Stoianoff, Blaze, private, Company H, 308th Infantry
Streshel, George, private, Company H, 308th Infantry
Strickland, James T., private, Company H, 308th Infantry, wounded
Stringer, Edward, private, Company E, 308th Infantry
Stromee, Leo A., captain, Company C, 308th Infantry, wounded
Strong, Len, private, Company B, 308th Infantry

Stumbe, Leroy A., private, Company K, 307th Infantry
Sugro, Benedetto, private, Company C, 308th Infantry
Summers, Alfred E., private, scout, Second Battalion, 308th Infantry
Sunby, Melvin G., private, Company H, 308th Infantry
Swanson, Edward, private, Company H, 308th Infantry
Swanson, Olaf W., private, Company E, 308th Infantry, killed
Swanson, Sigurd V., private, Company B, 308th Infantry
Swartz, John B., private, Company H, 308th Infantry, wounded
Sweeney, Bernard J., private, Company D, 306th Machine Gun
    Battalion, wounded

Taasaas, Andrew J., private, Company H, 308th Infantry
Tallon, Daniel V., private, Company E, 308th Infantry, killed
Teichmoeller, first lieutenant, Battery D, 305th Field Artillery
Ternquist, Benjamin E., private, Company K, 307th Infantry
Test, Pietro, private, Company K, 307th Infantry, wounded
Thomas, Clifford, private, Company K, 307th Infantry, wounded
Thomas, Harold H., private, Company H, 308th Infantry, killed
Thompson, Arthur A., corporal, Company D, 306th Machine Gun
    Battalion
Thompson, Charles, corporal, Company K, 307th Infantry
Thompson, Thomas J., private, Company D, 306th Machine Gun
    Battalion
Thorsen, Harry, private, runner, Second Battalion, 308th Infantry,
    wounded
Todesco, Amos, sergeant, Company G, 308th Infantry, wounded
Tollefson, Theodore, private, headquarters, First Battalion, 308th
    Infantry, missing
Tolley, Courtney W., private, Company D, 306th Machine Gun
    Battalion
Torpey, Leslie C., private, Company D, 306th Machine Gun Battalion
Trainor, Leo W., second lieutenant, Company C, 308th Infantry,
    wounded
Travers, John H., private, Company D, 306th Machine Gun
    Battalion, killed
Treadwell, Ray, private, Company K, 307th Infantry
Trigani, Antonio, private, Company G, 308th Infantry
Tucker, Jack, corporal, Company C, 308th Infantry
Tudor, Leonard, private, Company H, 308th Infantry

Tuite, Martin, private, Company C, 308th Infantry
Tulchin, David, private, Company C, First Battalion, 308th Infantry
Tumm, Charles G., corporal, Company H, 308th Infantry, killed

Underhill, Lester, mechanic, Company K, 307th Infantry
Untereines, Hugo E., private, Company H, 308th Infantry

Velz, Otto, private, Company K, 307th Infantry, wounded
Vitkus, Joseph, private, Company E, 308th Infantry
Vitulli, Constantine, private, Company C, 308th Infantry, wounded
Voorheis, John L., private, Company C, 308th Infantry

Wade, Farland F., private, Company G, 308th Infantry, wounded
Wallace, Dosia W., private, Company G, 308th Infantry
Wallen, Oscar, private, Company G, 308th Infantry, wounded
Wallenstein, Charles, private, Company C, 308th Infantry
Watkins, Richard, corporal, Company B, 308th Infantry
Weaver, Glenn H., private, Company G, 308th Infantry, wounded
Weiner, Walter, private, scout, Second Battalion, 308th Infantry
Welchel, Solomon, private, Company M, 308th Infantry
Wenzel, Edward L., private, scout, Second Battalion, 308th Infantry
Wheeler, Otto, private, Company H, 308th Infantry
White, Peter H., private, runner, Second Battalion, 308th Infantry
White, Scott R., private, Company H, 308th Infantry
Whiting, Wilbur C., corporal, Company H, 308th Infantry
Whitmarsh, Merle, private, Company K, 307th Infantry
Whittlesey, Charles W., major, First Battalion, 308th Infantry
Wilber, Frederick L., private, Company G, 308th Infantry, wounded
Williams, William, private, Company G, 308th Infantry
Williamson, Henry J., second lieutenant, Company A, 308th
    Infantry
Willinger, Isadore, private, Company K, 307th Infantry, missing
Willis, Oscar, private, Company H, 308th Infantry, wounded
Witschen, Vincent, private, Company K, 307th Infantry
Wolf, Samuel, Company D, 308th Infantry
Wondowlesky, Stephen, private, Company A, 308th Infantry
Woods, James R., private, Company G, 308th Infantry
Workman, William J., private, Company H, 308th Infantry, killed
Worneck, Ernest, private, Company G, 308th Infantry, wounded

Wright, William J., private, Company D, 306th Machine Gun
  Battalion

Zeman, Lewis, private, Company H, 308th Infantry, killed
Zieganbalg, William, private, Company B, 308th Infantry
Zizzo, Gasper, private, Company H, 308th Infantry, wounded

notes

Chapter One. Causes

1. See Donald Smythe, *Guerrilla Warrior: The Early Life of John J. Pershing* (New York: Scribner's, 1973). Also his *Pershing: General of the Armies* (Bloomington: Indiana University Press, 1988). Another biography is Frank E. Vandiver, *Black Jack: The Life and Times of John J. Pershing*, 2 vols. (Fort Worth: Texas Christian University Press, 1977).

2. Confidential reports, box 23, John J. Pershing papers, entry 22, record group 200. All citations followed by record group numbers are to the National Archives, College Park, Maryland. Harbord to McAndrew, January 31, 1919, James G. Harbord papers, manuscript division, Library of Congress.

3. Major General George B. Duncan disliked Alexander—for when Duncan had commanded the Seventy-seventh and was relieved for medical reasons, Alexander came in and claimed he had rescued the division from being turned into a depot (replacement) division because of its low state of readiness. Alexander made the claim in *Memories of the World War: 1917–1918* (New York: Macmillan, 1931). Duncan pronounced the memoir "the most blatant self sufficiency of utterance I have ever seen recorded by any responsible commander." Alexander's remarks about how he brought the division to readiness "produced a general guffaw from those who know him, for no matter how highly General Alexander rated his own services it was not so meritorious in the eyes of his superior commanders as to warrant the award to him of the Distinguished Service Medal" ("Reminiscences of the World War," 114–15, courtesy of Edward M. Coffman). General Pershing and army and corps commanders customarily awarded the D.S.M. to any commander who was above average. Thus, it differed from the Distinguished Service Cross, awarded for heroism.

4. Nelson M. Holderman, "Operations of the Force Known as 'The Lost Battalion,' from October 2nd to October 7th, 1918, Northeast of Binarville, in the Forest of Argonne, France," Fort Benning paper, 1924–1925. A copy is in the Seventy-seventh Division historical file, entry 1241, RG 120. Three copies are in boxes 236–37, American Battle Monuments Commission file, RG 117.

5. Jennifer D. Keene of Chapman University discovered this documentation in Mission militaire française près la 92nd DIUS, rapport du Capitaine de Metz Noblat sur les combats auxquels pris part la 92nd DIUS, Oct. 5, 1918, Serie 17N138, service historique de l'Armée de terre, Château de Vincennes, Paris.

6. "I speak French fluently; from conversation in the French P.C. that afternoon and evening and from a talk on the Rhine afterward with Colonel Durand whom I knew very well. I am of the opinion that the cause of the withdrawal was due to a lack of confidence in the colored troops on the part of the French command" (correspondence, Ninety-second Division, box 258, American Battle Monuments Commission file, RG 117).

Chapter Two. October 2–3

1. This is unclear in Alexander, *Memories of the World War*, 207–11.

2. "At this time it was stated the French had taken Lançon, and the 153d Brigade was in advance of my position. As a matter of fact neither was the case. The 153d Brigade was actually and relatively very much in my rear, for according to that advance they should have been in my front, while the French, far from being in Lançon, were five or six hundred meters to my left and rear as I knew from my liaison group, but I thought it probable the other French were in advance" (Captain Rich to inspector, First Army, Seventy-seventh Division, GHQ administrative staff, October 8, 1918, inspector general reports, box 1, entry 590, RG 120).

3. In many cases new company commanders asked their men which of them had been in the Lost Battalion and what the names were of men they remembered who were still in hospitals. Confusions from such estimates are evident in the calculation for E Company of twenty-one men. Lieutenant Leak escaped from the enemy action of October 3 with eighteen men, and Lieutenant Wilhelm broke through to headquarters of the 308th with four.

4. This showed how poorly Alexander used his staff and how poor the reporting was from the bottom of the staff on up. The Seventy-seventh had been in combat, but the staff officers should have had a better feel for what troops were in the field. Alexander had a history of poor staff work. He was not Pershing's choice for command of the Seventy-seventh; the commander in chief had put General Duncan in command but had to relieve him because of illness.

5. L. Wardlaw Miles, *History of the 308th Infantry: 1917–1919* (New York: Putnam's, 1927), 50–51. The *New York Times Magazine* for Sunday, September 30, 1928, a few days before the tenth anniversary of the surrounding of the two battalions, reprinted the chapter. It was attributed to Whittlesey and McMurtry but written by Captain Edwin Lewis of the 308th. Whittlesey reviewed the chapter. See "Epic of the Lost Battalion," box 237, American Battle Monuments Commission File, RG117.

6. Thomas M. Johnson, "The Lost Battalion," *American Magazine* 108 (November 1929): 55. See also Thomas M. Johnson and Fletcher Pratt, *The Lost Battalion* (Indianapolis: Bobbs-Merrill, 1938).

7. Richard Wellmann, *Das 1. Reserve-Korps in der Letzten Schlacht* (Hannover: Edler and Krasche, 1924).

8. Taylor V. Beattie, "Ghosts of the Lost Battalion," *Military History* (August 2002): 26–32. Another version by the same author, with notes, is "Whittlesey's Lost Battalion," *Army History* 54 (winter 2000): 21–30.

9. Miles, *History of the 308th Infantry*, shows Company A's strength as 18, G's as 56. A later captain of Company A, Barclay McFadden, brought together an account of what happened to the company after the beginning of the Meuse-Argonne. On September 26 it had 205 officers and men. On October 2, the beginning of the advance into the pocket, it was down to 106. A sergeant and two men were able to walk out of the pocket. Six other men of Company A survived the pocket, having been taken out. Afterward, men who had been detached for runners and other tasks returned, increasing company strength to seventy, this before replacements. Joseph P. Demaree, *History of Company A (308th Infantry) of the Lost Battalion* (New York: Harvey, 1920), 75–78.

10. All quotations of pigeon messages are from the chapter on the Lost Battalion in Miles, *History of the 308th Infantry*. Whittlesey's dispatch book came into the possession of A. Felix du Pont of E. I. du Pont de Nemours, who copied its contents and sent it to the colonel; the latter acknowledged receipt of it. Given to du Pont by a soldier, the book contained only three messages, which differed in minor detail from those in the Miles book (Du Pont to adjutant general, October 2, 1928, 277–32.16, "Epic of the Lost Battalion," box 237, American Battle Monuments Commission File, RG117.

11. Holderman, "Operations of the Force Known as 'The Lost Battalion,'" 42.

12. Johnson and Pratt, *Lost Battalion,* 109.

13. Lewis, "The Lost Battalion," box 237, American Battle Monuments Commission File, RG117. Lewis's essay in Miles, *History of the 308th Infantry,* does not contain this roll call.

14. Holderman, "Operations of the Force Known as 'The Lost Battalion,'" 21.

Chapter Three. October 4–5

1. Information courtesy James J. Cooke. The Civil War soldier stuffed his trousers into his socks. World War II had the combat boot.

2. Holderman, "Operations of the Force Known as 'The Lost Battalion,'" 26.

3. "Report of investigation of alleged wild firing by the 306th Field Artillery on Hill 212, France, October 6–7, 1918," folder 506, Seventy-seventh Division, general correspondence, G-3, GHQ, box 3101, entry 267, RG 120.

4. Johnson and Pratt, *Lost Battalion,* 135–36.

5. "Lost Battalion: Trial of Lt. Revnes," box 16, Hugh A. Drum papers, U.S. Army Military History Institute, Carlisle Barracks, Carlisle, Pa. The trial report has no pagination.

6. Whittlesey's after-action report of October 9, 1918, "Report of 1st and 2nd B'ns. 308th Infty from Oct. 2nd to Oct. 7th 1918," is also in 277.33.6, box 27, Seventy-seventh Division historical, entry 1241, RG 120.

7. "Lost Battalion: Trial of Lt. Revnes."

8. Two-plane Air Service missions went out on Saturday, October 5, both morning and afternoon. In addition to dropping messages, they dropped all available chocolate and cigarettes. One mission failed to notify division headquarters, Seventy-seventh Division, at Varennes, where two balloons were tied near the drop area using a message drop. Balloon cables had brought down an Air Service plane on the St. Mihiel front. "History of the Air Service (compiled by Colonel Gorrell)," Fiftieth Aero Squadron, series E, vol. 8, p. 96, box 27, RG 120.

9. Box 16, Drum papers.

10. Johnson and Pratt, *Lost Battalion,* 127.

11. "Lost Battalion: Trial of Lt. Revnes."

Chapter Four. The Gathering Solutions

1. See 277–66.1, box 18, Seventy-seventh Division historical, entry 1241, RG 120. See Appendix Two.

2. Alexander, *Memories of the World War,* 211.

3. "Brief history in the case of Colonel Cromwell Stacey, 308th Infantry," box 9, Pershing papers.

4. John C. H. Lee, "Service Reminiscences," U.S. Army Military History Institute.

5. For the Baer diary entry see box 3410, inspector general file, GHQ, RG 120.

6. See 277–32.16, message from General Alexander through Captain Whelpley, box 16, Seventy-seventh Division historical, entry 1241, RG 120.

7. Johnson to Pershing, April 19, 1921, folder 3, box 7, Pershing papers.

8. "Called on General Wittenmyer, commanding general of 7th, who seems pretty well satisfied with his command. He is sore at Alexander, of 77th, and thinks Evan Johnson untruthful" (Pierpont L. Stackpole diary, April 6, 1919, courtesy of Larry I. Bland). Duncan's appraisal is in "Reminiscences of the World War," 106.

9. See Appendix One.

10. Stackpole diary, October 5, 1918.

11. For the story of the Thirty-fifth, see my *Collapse at Meuse-Argonne: The Failure of the Missouri-Kansas Division* (Columbia: University of Missouri Press, 2004).

12. Stackpole diary, October 6–7, 1918.

13. *Official History of the 82nd Division, American Expeditionary Forces* (Indianapolis: Bobbs-Merrill, 1919), 39–40.

Chapter Five. October 6–7

1. "Lost Battalion: Trial of Lt. Revnes," summary in box 16, Drum papers.

2. Box 16, Drum papers.

3. "History of the Air Service (compiled by Colonel Gorrell)," Fiftieth Aero Squadron, series E, vol. 8, pp. 96–98, box 27, RG 120.

4. In 1927 a reporter, James B. Wharton, found and interviewed Prinz in Cassel. The interview appeared in the *Washington Star* on May 1 under the heading "German Story of 'Lost Battalion' Is Answered by Americans." General Alexander and Lieutenant William J. Cullen commented, Alexander contending that Major Whittlesey was not in error in allowing his force to be surrounded.

5. Box 16, Drum papers.

6. Johnson and Pratt, *Lost Battalion,* 304.

7. Ibid., 274.

8. Ibid., 248.

9. Laurence Stallings, *The Doughboys: The Story of the AEF, 1917–1918* (New York: Harper and Row, 1963), 275.

10. Box 16, Drum papers.

11. Ibid.

12. Lee C. McCollum, *History and Rhymes of the Lost Battalion* (n.p., 1919), 84–85.

13. Holderman, "Operations of the Force Known as 'The Lost Battalion,'" 35; W. Kerr Rainsford, *From Upton to the Meuse: With the Three Hundred and Seventh Infantry* (New York: Appleton, 1920), 222.

14. "Lost Battalion: Trial of Lt. Revnes."

Chapter Six. Aftermath

1. Holderman, "Operations of the Force Known as 'The Lost Battalion,'" 37; Hurley E. Fuller, "'Lost Battalion' of the 77th Division," *Infantry Journal* 28 (June 1926): 608.

2. Johnson to Pershing, April 19, 1921, folder 3, box 7, Pershing papers.

3. Box 16, Drum papers.

4. See the Military History Institute survey for First Corps.

5. For Whittlesey's disappearance and aftermath, see *New York Times*, November 29–30, December 1–4, 6, 9, 14–15, 18–19, 1921.

6. Ibid., September 4, 1953.

7. Ibid., November 24, 1958.

8. Ibid., August 27, 1941; October 14, 1923.

Appendix One. General Johnson's Protest

1. From 277–32.16, box 16, Seventy-seventh Division historical, entry 1241, RG 120.

Appendix Two. General Johnson's Request for Relief

1. From 277–66.1, box 18, Seventy-seventh Division historical, entry 1241, RG 120.

Appendix Three. Roster of the Lost Battalion

1. The copy used to compile the roster that follows is in "The Lost Battalion," general correspondence, folder 2154-A, box 3226, G-3 reports, GHQ, RG 120.

sources

Considering that the Lost Battalion inspired more newspaper copy than any other event or any other action during the American participation in World War I, from April 6, 1917, to November 11, 1918, it is surprising that the printed literature is so scarce on what happened when the six companies of the 308th Infantry, Holderman's company of the 307th, and two sections of the 306th Machine Gun Battalion went into the pocket. Newspaper stories were legion, in every paper across the country, large and small, and they were speculated upon, with lessons drawn, by every editor who put his Linotype or other typesetting equipment to the task. But the books—one would have thought they would be at least a dozen, perhaps two—did not appear. There were only a few, and they were, unfortunately, not worthy of the valor of the surrounded men over the five days of siege.

The first of the books, really a pamphlet—brought out by a private in the 308th Regiment, Lee C. McCollum, who knew that if he could produce something resembling a book it would sell—celebrated Krotoshinsky's escape from the pocket. Entitled *History and Rhymes of the Lost Battalion* (n.p., 1919), it proved immensely successful; a printing of 1929 showed 700,000 copies. Krotoshinsky's account, assisted by the editor, was probably accurate in terms of what happened when he got out of the pocket but unbelievable in its claim that on his way to the 307th Infantry he was hiding when a German officer (not a soldier) stepped on his hand. The booklet offered other testimonies and documents, enough to bulk it out.

The first account that touched authoritatively on the Lost Battalion was a history of the 307th Infantry by a company commander who, wounded in the Oise-Aisne offensive, was barely in any of the action involving the Lost Battalion. This was W. Kerr Rainsford, *From Upton to the Meuse: With the Three Hundred and Seventh Infantry* (New York: Appleton, 1920). Rainsford took part in the first attempts to relieve the men, was wounded once more, and returned to duty in December. A Harvard graduate who in 1911 attended the École des Beaux Arts in Paris and in 1917 participated in an officers' training camp at Plattsburg, New York, one of the camps instituted by General Wood that trained hundreds of civilians as officers, Rainsford possessed the talents for a regimental historian.

The history of the 308th was told by L. Wardlaw Miles in *History of the 308th Infantry: 1917–1919* (New York: Putnam's, 1927). Captain Miles of the 308th received the Congressional Medal of Honor for an action on September 14, 1918, during the St. Mihiel battle. The book contained a chapter attributed to Whittlesey and McMurtry but written by Captain Edwin Lewis of the 308th.

It seems strange, but it happened, that the next book did not appear until 1938. This was Thomas M. Johnson and Fletcher Pratt, *The Lost Battalion* (Indianapolis: Bobbs-Merrill). It offered information gathered apparently from every possible source—from participants, to be sure, many of whom were alive at that time, in their midforties, and from what the authors described as "official records." The authors' credentials were unexceptionable. Johnson had been a war reporter in 1917–1918 and was present on October 8 in the Charlevaux valley when Whittlesey led the men out of the pocket. He published "The Lost Battalion," *American Magazine* 108 (November, 1929): 54–57, 80, 82, 84, 86, a finely written piece. Pratt was a military historian, the author of many books, including after World War II an account of that war in the Chronicles of America series published by Yale University Press, used by college and university teachers to supplement their lectures.

Unfortunately, Johnson and Pratt's book was poorly researched. The factual errors in Johnson's account in *American Magazine* were many—they were small errors, but ones that showed indifference to detail—and there were many more in the book of 1938. One has the impression that Pratt relied on Johnson for material and may not have looked closely at what he received. The same held for the participants' accounts in the book, some of which came from newspaper stories of varied authenticity. A reader cannot know whether something offered as fact was true or otherwise, accepted by the authors to enliven their story.

The book contains a glaring error of geography, in its description of a hill in the subsector of the First Division in the Meuse-Argonne, Montrefagne, on which lay the Bois de Boyon, below which was the village of Exermont. Johnson and Pratt placed the Montrefagne south of Exermont. During the attack in the Meuse-Argonne beginning on September 26, Exermont was the farthest point the Thirty-fifth Division managed to reach, on September 29. From there the division's men, numbering little more than a hundred, too weak a force to hold, went back, with terrible losses going and returning. The First Division had to retake the village and take the hill. All this was lost on Johnson and Pratt.

A later book was Irving Werstein's *The Lost Battalion* (New York: Norton, 1966). The author of a dozen or so accounts of battles on land or sea, Werstein wrote briskly and carelessly. He copied the error about Montrefagne in Johnson and Pratt's work, almost word for word.

For readers wishing to know what happened to the Lost Battalion, the only recourse must be to manuscript materials. This means, first of all, the records housed at the U.S. Army Military History Institute, a part of the Army War College at Carlisle Barracks, Carlisle, Pennsylvania. The institute holds papers of the army's officers and men, in two files. One is by name, begun many years ago, and includes individuals in actions and campaigns from 1775. As one might expect, it is weak on early material, picking up for the Mexican War, strong on the Civil War, fairly strong thereafter including World Wars I and II and Vietnam. The other file is a survey, a massive collection of questionnaires and papers—diaries, memoirs, letters—assembled by the institute beginning a generation ago. Organized by general headquarters, army, corps, and divisions, with the latter organized by brigades, regiments, and companies, the survey contains a mixture of the important and trivial. The questionnaires, sent out to mailing lists of veterans' organizations and to those who responded to advertisements in journals and periodicals read by veterans, were not very successful ventures for World War I, for by the 1970s the veterans were aging, their memories unclear, and they

marked questionnaires hurriedly, lingering on queries as to their favorite songs. But the survey brought in papers, often saved from the
dumpsters where they would have been placed by relatives dispos-
ing of them upon veterans' illnesses and deaths. The Military History Institute holds the nation's best collection of unit histories.

The other resort for the Lost Battalion, as on all other actions and
wars of the last century (eighteenth- and nineteenth-century records are in the old National Archives building at Seventh and
Pennsylvania in Washington, D.C.), is the huge new archives building in College Park, Maryland, three or four miles from the University of Maryland's main campus—the university donated the
land, virtually in the country, for the building constructed in the
1990s, a gleaming behemoth of glass. Within are miles of stacks con-
taining documents, in Hollinger boxes five inches wide, filed verti-
cally, or for World War II and after (not to mention all other records
apart from military, of cabinet departments and special agencies)
larger containers with lids. A sizable search room enables researchers
to work at four-person tables, with boxes brought out on library
trucks several times daily to enable the reading and copying of documents.

Records for the AEF in World War I appear to have come back in
considerable disorder, as shipping afforded, but archivists in the early
1920s organized them. Basic records are by division, for the Lost
Battalion in a file known as "Seventy-seventh Division historical."
Thereafter the resort is to files of First Corps, First Army, and General Headquarters, and to such special files as those of the American Battle Monuments Commission, a group created in the middle
and later 1920s, headed by General Pershing, which sought accurate
accountings of what happened in France. Officers wrote not merely
to Regular officers but also to participants returned to civil life, sending maps and draft accounts and asking for confirmation or correc-
tion.

An account from the German side can be found in Richard Wellmann, *Das 1. Reserve-Korps in der Letzten Schlacht* (Hannover: Edler
and Krasche, 1924).

Index